HS 362.3 WAhS

Women with Disabilities Aging Well

A Global View

Patricia Noonan Walsh, Ph.D.
Centre for Disabilities Studies
University College Dublin
Ireland

Barbara LeRoy, Ph.D.
Developmental Disabilities Institute
Wayne State University
Detroit, Michigan

·P A U L·H·
BROOKES
PUBLISHING CO.®

Baltimore • London • Sydney

Paul H. Brookes Publishing Co.
Post Office Box 10624
Baltimore, MD 21285-0624

www.brookespublishing.com

Typeset by Auburn Associates, Inc., Baltimore, Maryland.
Manufactured in the United States of America by
Versa Press, East Peoria, Illinois.

All examples and quotations in this book are based on the authors' and contributors' actual experiences and used by permission.

Lines from "Delta" (p. 79). Copyright © 2002, 1989 by Adrienne Rich, from THE FACT OF A DOORFRAME: SELECTED POEMS 1950–2001 by Adrienne Rich. Used by permission of the author and W.W. Norton & Company, Inc.

Lines from "Quilting" (p. 125). Copyright © 2000 by Lucille Clifton, from BLESSING THE BOATS: NEW AND SELECTED POEMS 1988–2000 by Lucille Clifton. Used by permission of the author and BOA Editions, Ltd.

Library of Congress Cataloging-in-Publication Data
Walsh, Patricia Noonan.
    Women with disabilities aging well: a global view / by Patricia Noonan Walsh and Barbara LeRoy.
        p.   cm.
    Includes bibliographic references and index.
    ISBN 1-55766-715-2 (pdk: alk. paper)
    1. Women with mental disabilities—Health and hygiene—Cross-cultural studies.   2. Women with mental disabilities—Social conditions—Cross-cultural studies.   3. Aged women—Mental health—Cross-cultural studies.
4. Aging—Cross-cultural studies.
    [DNLM: 1. Mentally Disabled Persons—Aged—Personal Narratives. 2. Women—Personal Narratives. 3. Cross-Cultural Comparison—Personal Narratives. 4. Developmental Disabilities—Aged—Personal Narratives.
5. Quality of Life—Personal Narratives.
    HV 3009.5.W65 W226w 2004]   I. LeRoy, Barbara. II. Title.
RA 564.89.W356   2004
362.3'082—dc22   2004002553

British Library Cataloguing in Publication data are available from the British Library.

Women
with Disabilities
Aging Well

Contents

About the Authors

Patricia Noonan Walsh, Ph.D., is NDA Professor of Disability Studies at University College Dublin in Ireland and is a Fellow of The International Association for the Scientific Study of Intellectual Disability (IASSID). She has authored publications in the areas of aging, inclusive employment and education, and the health and quality of life of people with disabilities. Dr. Walsh is co-editor with Tamar Heller of *Health of Women with Intellectual Disabilities* (Blackwell, 2002).

Barbara LeRoy, Ph.D., is Director of the Developmental Disabilities Institute at Wayne State University in Detroit, Michigan. She received her doctorate in rehabilitation counseling from the University of Michigan. She is the author of publications in the areas of inclusive education, welfare reform, and women's issues. She is a governor's appointee to the Michigan Developmental Disabilities Council, a board member of the United States International Council on Disabilities (USICD), a delegate to the Education Commission of Rehabilitation International (RI), and a disability and education consultant to the Organisation for Economic Co-operation and Development (OECD).

About the Collaborators

Ms. Maarit Aalto is Project Secretary for the Association for the Welfare of the Swedish-Speaking Mentally Retarded (FDUV), a Finnish interest organization for parents of children, young people, and adults who have intellectual disabilities. Her responsibility in the organization is to take care of national and international research and development projects concerning such themes as power use and deinstitutionalization, quality of services, community-based settings, methods for social development, aging people with intellectual disabilities, and aging parents of people with intellectual disabilities living at home.

Dr. Christine Bigby is Senior Lecturer and Director of Undergraduate Programs in the School of Social Work and Social Policy at LaTrobe University in Melbourne, Australia. Her main research interest is the transition from parental care and successful aging for middle-age and older adults with intellectual disabilities.

Ms. Monique Bochirol is trained in special education, and she worked with adults with intellectual disabilities for 9 years before becoming head of one of France's first group homes for aging people with intellectual disabilities. She worked there for 14 years, during which she earned several university degrees in gerontology. She currently works as a teacher in a training college for social workers.

Ms. Nancy Breitenbach has been involved in disability and human rights issues on a number of levels: as a researcher of dramatherapy with children, as Grant Officer in charge of disability programs at the Fondation de France (where she launched a 10-year program on aging), and as Chief Executive Officer of Inclusion International. She is currently an international disability consultant specializing in aging.

Ms. Maaike Canrinus is currently completing a master's degree in clinical psychology at University of Guelph in Ontario, Canada.

Dr. Chris Conliffe is Director of the Institute for Counselling and Personal Development in Belfast and Professor in the School of Psychology at the University of Ulster. Professor Conliffe is Scientific Adviser to the European Down Syndrome Association and founded the Institute for Counselling and Personal Development in 1985, which offers free counseling service throughout Northern Ireland. Dr. Conliffe has published books and articles on topics that include caring, aging, disability, and human rights.

Ms. Marcella DeLuca has been an analyst at the Center for Education Research and Innovation in France, part of the Organisation for Economic Co-operation and Development (OECD), since 1998. She has published a number of articles in the social science periodical *Percorsi di Integrazione*, for which she also serves as a member of the editorial staff. Since 1991, she has served as Project Coordinator, Press Agent, and Public Relations Officer for a European Union program called EURIDICE, which tracks drug addiction in the workplace and provides proposals for intervention. Ms. DeLuca has a master of science degree in European social policy from the London School of Economics.

Ms. Angela Dew is a researcher in the Disability Studies Initiative in the Faculty of Health Sciences at the University of Sydney. She comes from a management position in disability services and has extensive experience researching community living and postinstitutional care for people with intellectual disabilities.

Ms. Natacha Glautier works as a researcher for the European Association of Service Providers for People with Disabilities in Brussels. She has a master's degree in psychological and educational sciences, specialized in special education, and focuses on disability issues. Since 2002, she has worked as Project Leader on issues regarding the aging of people with intellectual disabilities, community-based settings, and deinstitutionalization of services.

Ms. Florence Hermouet-Imbert worked in a special setting for older people with intellectual disabilities for 5 years, which led to her degree in gerontology. She now manages a group home for adults with severe intellectual disabilities in France. Since 1999, she has coordinated the Committee on Aging, part of the local Bureau on Disability, l'Office Départemental des Personnes Handicapées de l'Isère (ODPHI).

Ms. Susan Hunter is Lecturer in social work at the University of Edinburgh in Scotland, where she has lead responsibility for teaching in the areas of disability and aging. Her research interests include evaluation of resettlement and reprovisioning initiatives, supported living, and independent advocacy. She has chaired a number of innovative organizations working in the field of disability including Scottish Human Services Trust (SHS), Key Housing Association and Community Lifestyles, and the Edinburgh Development Group.

Dr. Kristjana Kristiansen is Associate Professor at the Norwegian University of Science and Technology in Trondheim, where she teaches research methods, gender studies, and disability studies at the postgraduate level in health and social sciences. She is also Secretary of the Board of the Nordic Network for Disability Research and has research interests in social marginalization, participatory-action research, and societal/cultural understandings of disability and mental health.

Ms. Joan Lesseliers is a researcher and doctoral student in the Department of Special Education of Ghent University in Belgium. She has been researching the relational and sexual experiences of people with learning disabilities. In 2002, she helped a European Service Providers Association (EASPD) to establish the European Knowledge Centre for the Prevention of and Response to Sexual Abuse of People with a Learning Disability.

Dr. Gwynnyth Llewellyn is Director of the Family Support Services Project and Disability Studies Initiative in the Faculty of Health Sciences at the University of Sydney in Australia. She writes regularly on family and disability topics, including parenting by people with intellectual disabilities.

Dr. Yona Lunsky is Assistant Professor in the University of Toronto's Department of Psychiatry. She is also Psychologist in the Dual Diagnosis Program at the Centre for Addiction and Mental Health in Canada.

Dr. Maria del Carmen Malbran is an educational psychologist and a senior teacher and researcher in the field of cognitive psychology. She teaches undergraduate and postgraduate courses at the University of Buenos Aires and the National University of La Plata in Argentina. In addition, Dr. Malbran is a member of The National Council of Scientific Research on Technology (CONICET) in Argentina. She is a council member of The International Association for the Scientific Study of Intellectual Disability (IASSID). Her research and teaching areas include cognitive diversity, inclusive education, and development of cognitive processes and abilities.

Ms. Ali O'Callaghan is a lecturer in learning disability at the University of Kent, Canterbury, in the United Kingdom. Her particular research interests are capacity to consent, sexuality, and abuse issues.

Dr. Julie Ridley is an independent research and development consultant working in the field of health and community care research in Scotland.

Ms. Margaret Rooney has worked in the Irish health care environment since 1984, focusing on the support, management, planning, and commissioning of client services and programs that include services for people with disabilities, older adults, and children. She previously worked in Services Management at Our Lady's Hospital for Sick Children in Dublin and as Day Services Manager at Moore Abbey in Kildare. She is currently Director of family support services at St. Anne's Centre, Roscrea. Ms. Rooney has a particular interest in the life experiences and views of women with intellectual disabilities as they age. She holds a master of science degree in developmental disabilities from University College Dublin.

Dr. Ryo Takahashi is Lecturer at the Takasaki University of Health and Welfare in Japan. He graduated from Sendai College, majoring in physical education. He then studied at the Jouetsu University of Education's Graduate School, receiving a master's degree in special education for children and adults with intellectual disabilities. After that, he studied at the University of Utah's Graduate School of Education in a doctoral course specializing in special education and gerontology.

Dr. Kuo-yu Wang is Associate Professor in the Department of Social Welfare at National Chung Cheng University in Taiwan. She has been a council member and Fellow of The International Association for the Scientific Study of Intellectual Disabilities (IASSID) since 2000, through which she actively coordinates the regional organization of IASSID in the Pacific Region. Locally, she worked closely with the Parents Association for People with Intellectual Disabilities (PAPID) to advocate health services and care issues for adults with intellectual disabilities. Both her research and advocacy work allow her to transfer research results into policy.

Dr. Olive J. Webb is a clinical psychologist who has worked in the area of intellectual disability for more than 30 years, specializing in people who have both mental illness and intellectual disabilities. Currently, she works as a health and disability consultant to IHC New Zealand, Inc., and to the New Zealand–based Richmond Fellowship. She has been central to the deinstitutionalization movement in New Zealand. She has published widely in the field of intellectual disability, focusing on sexual education, challenging and offending behavior by people with intellectual disabilities, and various aspects of health care for people with intellectual disabilities.

Dr. Germain Weber is Professor in the Department of Psychology, Unit Clinical and Health Psychology of the University of Vienna, where he teaches courses in clinical and rehabilitation psychology. Dr. Weber also serves as Director of the postgraduate training program for clinical and health psychology at the University of Vienna. He is Vice President of the Lebenshilfe Österreich, the major Austrian parents' organization serving for and advocating on behalf of people with intellectual disabilities, and of the Österreichische Arbeitsgemeinschaft für Rehabilitation, the Austrian umbrella organization of disability associations. In 2000, Dr. Weber's contributions to the field of intellectual disability were honored with the International Award offered by the American Association on Mental Retardation.

Ms. Maria Amelia Vampré Xavier is Director of International Affairs with the Federação Nacional das Associação de Pais e Amigos dos Excepcionais de São Paulo (APAE-SP) in Brazil.

Foreword

Not long ago, a man who was purported to be the world's oldest man died in Japan at age 114. The world's oldest woman, at age 116, was living nearby and at the time was still doing well. (She has since died.) These events are telling, for they reflect three emerging demographic issues prevalent in the developed world: Women tend to outlive men, longevity is increasing throughout the world, and the health status of older people in general is better. They also raise some questions: What is the quality of life of older women? To what extent is increased longevity prevalent among women with lifelong disabilities? What are their lives like?

Women with Disabilities Aging Well: A Global View is a welcome addition to the growing literature on issues facing people as they age because it addresses an area too often neglected within the focus on positive aging—growing older with a lifelong disability. Much of the extant aging research and literature has ignored the needs of women with disabilities and has not offered insights into their particular challenges and the means many have used to overcome their problems. This text recognizes the nuanced issues important to the social and physical health of older women with disabilities.

Dr. Patricia Noonan Walsh and Dr. Barbara LeRoy, the authors, have done an outstanding job of assembling a text that will resonate well internationally among workers concerned with the welfare of older women with lifelong disabilities. In this seminal text, Walsh and LeRoy have aptly laid out the issues and arguments that illuminate an emerging trend—the partnering of experiences from diverse cultures and perspectives that help frame an issue integral to aging—and help readers better understand these universal aspects as they are applied to the field of disability research. Both authors are skilled and respected researchers and authors in the area of intellectual disabilities and bring their knowledge of this issue and the breadth of their network to the stories told by the women whose lives make up this text. Books on the topic of sex differences among potentially devalued people are beginning to emerge, but this is the first such text to be based on the personal reflections and experiences of the people being written about. Given the way that the women's stories have framed the issues raised in the text, it will no doubt become an invaluable aid to policy makers, families, advocates, researchers, and others whose quest is increased comprehension of the nature of disability and improvement of the lives of the people affected by it.

This text provides us with a grand tour of challenges that women with lifelong disabilities face daily, and drawing from the experiences of the women themselves, it begins to give us a basis for better understanding of what these women face, how they perceive their aging, and what strategies they employ to cope with their life situations. Both authors, skilled and experienced in the facets of disability and aging, have used their collective knowledge to expand on the lifespan challenges of women with disabilities and to illuminate the ways in which these women manage their lives and strive toward healthier aging and increased longevity.

The World Health Organization (WHO), charged by the United Nations to promote issues related to our collective populations' health status, reported on women's health and aging as it relates to women with intellectual and developmental disabilities. Most telling in that report was the notation that "[T]he distinctive needs, vulnerabilities, and sources of well-being for women with intellectual disabilities must be addressed vigorously." WHO further noted, "Promoting women's health across the life-span needs to be seen as part of a global strategy." This text will go far in addressing this challenge and providing researchers, families, public officials, and women with disabilities with a compendium of information that they can use. I commend Walsh and LeRoy for their effort and envision this text playing a integral and useful role in framing public policy internationally and stimulating new research in an heretofore neglected area of concern.

Matthew P. Janicki, Ph.D.
University of Illinois at Chicago

REFERENCE

World Health Organization. (2000). *Ageing and intellectual disability: Improving longevity and promoting healthy ageing.* Geneva: Author.

Acknowledgments

This book would not have been possible without the dedication and hard work of our collaborators around the world. They willingly took on the difficult task of recruiting, interviewing, and in many instances, translating the stories of older women with intellectual disabilities in their native countries. We thank them for believing in our mission of listening to the voices of these women and in trying to bring those voices to light in the hearts and minds of families, care providers, and policy makers.

We also want to acknowledge and thank our tireless research assistants on both sides of the Atlantic: Richard Molloy and Christine Linehan in Ireland and Noel Kulik, Angela Martin, and Nathaniel Israel in the United States. Without them, this book would surely not have come to fruition.

We also thank the Wayne State University Offices of the Vice President for Academic Affairs and the Vice President for Research and Sponsored Programs, who provided financial assistance to ensure that our international collaborators and American study participants were paid for their contributions.

*To the 167 women who so
willingly told us the stories of their lives
and who continue, in spite of many obstacles,
to do as one Norwegian woman described:*

"dream of summer"

CHAPTER ONE

Introduction

Yesterday in a rural village in Taiwan, Huang, a widow in her fifties, rose just after 7:00 in the small home she owns and shares with three of her four children. She took a walk after breakfast—she has a good appetite, eats most foods, and does not take any regular medication. As usual, she cycled to carry out her day's work. Cycling and walking are her main forms of exercise. The money she earns from collecting boxes and waste paper for recycling supplements her income. In addition, she receives a government disability allowance, contributions from her children, and a survivor's pension, as her husband was a soldier. She does not worry about being alone or uncared for in the days to come because she feels her children will always be around. Yesterday was much the same as all of the other days since her husband's death a few years ago. She rates her own health as good, and overall she feels happy. She can see her children every day, so she does not feel lonely.

Yesterday in a town in Norway, Kristin awoke in the group home she shares with three housemates. As usual, she washed, dressed, and prepared breakfast. Later, like her counterpart in Taiwan, she took a walk. Kristin walks more slowly these days. She wears a hearing aid and uses earphones to listen to the radio. She did some knitting, went window-shopping, and watched television after supper. Kristin talked to her friends, washed her hair, and tidied her room before going to bed. She says she has "trouble understanding" and supposes that the phrase *intel-*

lectual disability best describes her major difficulty. Kristin relies on others: a home helper, staff living nearby, and neighbors. Although she receives a regular government social insurance benefit, she does not know what her annual income is.

Kristin was born in a rural area nearly 60 years ago and recalls her early years doing farm work and babysitting. The best aspects about this were "being outside in the summer [and] doing important things." The worst was that that it was heavy, often dirty, work. Kristin left home early:

> After 12 years, I was in an institution and visited them [my family] at holiday times, and they visited me. It was sad to be away from them, especially when they took my daughter away. Friends and staff were nice when my father died. Sad when they took my daughter away, but everyone said it was good for her.

When asked what the secret to her life is, she is not sure but says, "Now I know I am okay, like normal." She wonders about the future:

> Maybe when I get older I can no longer live here because of the stairs and I live on the second floor. To live alone or to have my daughter live with me, but that is a dream.

Separated by geography and culture, one more reticent, the other more voluble, these two women with intellectual disabilities have each shaped a successful life for nearly six decades. Huang relied on an early marriage to lend status and protection, and she has never used formal support services. Rather, she intends to live with her adult children, and they are her main supports now and, she suggests, in the years ahead. Even now, she works to contribute to her own and her family's livelihood. In Norway, Kristin has a long history of involvement with various health, social, and housing agencies and lived for many years in an institution. She, too, is a parent, but she was separated from her child many years ago. That child will play no part in her mother's old age. Millions of women like Huang and Kristin spent the day yesterday engaged with parents, siblings and other kin, friends, neighbors, or professional support workers. A small number, 167, are represented in this book. Yesterday, some attended sheltered workshops in France, Belgium, Ireland; nearly all of these women are single. Many women were otherwise occupied—they traveled by ferry to an advocacy meeting in New Zealand, helped to care for young children in the family home in Argentina, worked in a small shop in Finland, went out for shopping and afternoon tea in Scotland. Women in Norway regarded the winter landscape, recalling their youth on skis and dreaming of the summer to come.

This book tries to capture different facets of experience: being an individual woman in late middle and older adulthood, being identified as having a disability, being a member of a distinctive culture, having been born during the middle decades of the 20th century. Older women recall the Second World War and even their parents' accounts of the First World War. Younger women are mindful of current affairs in the Middle East. In this chapter, we adopt a global view to introduce the study, offering reasons why it is important to understand more about the experiences of growing older for women with intellectual disabilities. We mark the book's limitations and set the scene for the stories to follow.

A GLOBAL VIEW

How many women worldwide have intellectual disabilities? Is their status similar across countries? What are their family circumstances? Even now, answers to these essential questions remain unclear. First, it is estimated that about 10% of the world's population may have some sort of disability, and accordingly, it is expected that about 300 million women are in this group (World Health Organization, 2002). If between 1% and 3% of all individuals worldwide have intellectual or other developmental disabilities, then the two women in rural Taiwan and Norway belong to a cohort that is at least 30 million strong. And most of these women live in developing countries. It has been suggested that current patterns of gender bias in a few countries where adult women are estimated to be missing in the general population arose because women in those countries are less likely to live to maturity as the result of policies favoring the survival of boys (Sen, 1999). We cannot say with confidence whether there are fewer women than might otherwise be expected in this special population of people with intellectual disabilities.

Second, the absence of reliable data about the population of people with intellectual disabilities is linked to disparities in methods used to define and record the presence of individuals in this group. Countries vary markedly in their practices, even in an apparently homogenous region, such as Europe (see Chapter 3). Not all countries have the inclination or resources to carry out a national census of the general population, let alone a separate tally of individuals with disabilities. It is likely, too, that many women are simply invisible to official scrutiny in their countries. Those with a mild level of intellectual disabilities may grow to adulthood without being diagnosed and lead marginal lives shadowed by poverty, dependency, stigma, or seclusion. Cultural differences both stem from, and exert influence on, the ways in which disabilities are construed. Many social and economic factors contribute to local practices. Patterns of employment—as a consequence of labor migration, for example—may alter family composition if the breadwinners must leave home for long periods to seek employment. Their absence will in turn limit the capacity of a family to care for a member with a disability. One consequence may be a swelling demand for special programs for people with disabilities and thus a new social category in a culture in which such men and women had hitherto been unremarkable (Ingstad & Whyte, 1995).

Cultural expectations and practices are diverse. In a multinational study of attitudes, it was evident that the public opinion about whether individuals with intellectual disabilities should live with their families varied from country to country (Siperstein, Norrins, Corbin, & Shriver, 2003). In a very large survey with 8,000 participants in 10 countries, including the United States and Ireland, the vast majority of all surveyed believed that individuals with intellectual disabilities should attend special schools, and one third endorsed separate or sheltered workshops (Siperstein et al., 2003).

A historical survey of the status of people with disabilities reveals great diversity in how people are identified and what places they have taken up in their own cultures. Social constructions have affected the status of people with disabilities in different ways over the years. In much of Europe, for example, their treatment as cared for but marginalized people during the Middle Ages evolved into contemporary themes of rehabilitation and specialized institutions (Stiker, 1997). In the United States, the sheer size and number of regimented institutions during the 19th and 20th centuries grew alongside a corresponding conceptual process that Trent (1994) called "inventing the feeble mind." The tide in favor of large, separate institutions turned only relatively recently, and traces persist in many countries.

Within this global context, the identities and experiences of people with disabilities as men and women in their own societies have been muted. This muffled silence is perhaps most striking among older women with intellectual disabilities.

WOMEN WITH DISABILITIES

Each woman's life experience is unique and immediate. The personal domain is the center of a life that is available to public scrutiny and affected by economic and political forces within a given environmental context. Striving for their livelihoods and personal satisfaction as other women do, those with physical, sensory, or other disabilities nonetheless face tremendous barriers to equity of health care, economic status, and social participation. Their lower social status and levels of income in most countries are exacerbated by the disadvantage of experiencing disability, circumstances contrary to social justice (Fairchild, 2002). In some countries, women with disabilities may attract greater stigma than men and thus lead even more marginal and dependent lives (Hanna & Rogovsky, 1991).

Women in developing countries—where most people with intellectual disabilities live—encounter layers of disadvantage. For example, data suggest that gender inequity plays a role in the very high rates of pregnancy-related mortality and morbidity among women in less developed countries (Murphy, 2003). These factors include women's greater poverty and exclusion from decisions made about their own lives. The consequences of poverty, gender disadvantage, and disability accrue with age, making older women with intellectual disabilities especially vulnerable. As a consequence, women with disabilities in developing countries are at particular risk, although this population is as yet underresearched (Groce, 1997). Two forces—population aging and an emerging consensus that promoting quality of life is a desired goal—compel policy makers to address healthy aging of women with disabilities as a priority.

Aging

The impact of what Alvarez calls "the age-quake" will affect the lives of women and men in every country during the 21st century (Alvarez, 1999). These tremors will ripple through the lives of people with intellectual disabilities, their family members, and the society providing support to all (Fujiura, 2002; World Health Organization, 2000). Greater life expectancy and an increase in the population of people with intellectual disabilities are signs of a demographic sea change, bringing fresh challenges in its wake.

Drawing on cross-cultural data, Braddock and colleagues (2001) surveyed where people with intellectual disabilities currently live in five countries with developed service systems—Australia, Canada, England, the United States, and Wales. Nearly all children and many adults in these countries lived in family homes, but the likelihood of placement outside the family home rose steadily with adulthood and progressively so as adults aged. This pattern reflects one of the main challenges of transition in promoting a good quality of life on behalf of older people with intellectual disabilities (Janicki, 1997). Enabling people to grow old in place—that is, providing supports where they are rooted, content, and engaged with their own communities—is an ambition with wide appeal. But achieving it on behalf of the increasing number of men and women who become frail, who outlive their loved ones, who develop additional physical or sensorial difficulties, or who experience dementia will present vast challenges in coming years.

Healthy Aging of Women with Intellectual Disabilities

Among women with intellectual disabilities, this accrual of disadvantage may be manifested in a crucial domain of their lives—their health (Gill & Brown, 2002; Walsh, 2002). Women in this population have distinctive characteristics and also experience social practices and attitudes that affect their reproductive and sexual health (van Schrojenstein Lantman-de Valk, Schupf, & Patja, 2002). Understanding of their vulnerability to mental health difficulties (Lunsky & Havercamp, 2002), the factors related to risk of abuse (Walsh & Murphy, 2002), and the hallmarks of effective health promotion strategies on their behalf (Heller & Marks, 2002) is as yet incomplete.

In this book, we focus on the successful aging of women in this group in order to explore sources of resilience. Through a network of research collaborators in 18 countries, we invited the women themselves to speak about their defining moments, as well as ordinary days and years of their lives.

LIMITATIONS

This book limits its scope and size. Keeping our focus on lives lived from the inside out, we did not aim to select and describe a representative sample of women with intellectual disabilities around the globe. Rather, we drew a circle to include colleagues who knew their own territories most deeply and were committed to offering the women they knew an opportunity to speak about their lives.

Nor did we wish to devise a service system atlas ranking global regions according to how conducive a locality might be in promoting a good quality of life for people with intellectual disabilities. Although this book is international in scope, information from only about 1 in 10 of the world's countries was assembled to prepare this book. The selected countries vary a good deal in size, culture, language, climate, history, and political structures. Some of the Nordic countries, for example, were early settlers of the deinstitutionalization terrain, while others persist in a tradition of offering separate, custodial care for people with disabilities. Still others rely almost entirely on families for lifelong support of any members who have disabilities. And yet the 18 countries represented are among the more prosperous nations of the world in income and other measures of human development (see Chapter 3).

As we expected, our collaborators each had a unique story to tell about the status of people with intellectual disabilities in their countries. And each woman who took part exemplified in some way how these diverse systems of support and practice had evolved over time. We found, for example, that what was perceived as the typical form of daily occupation had many guises. While some women held one or even two paying jobs in the open labor market, others attended sheltered workshops for a token wage. A few contributed to their own livelihoods by working alongside family members as best they could—farming, cleaning, trading, or caring for relatives' young children. Some found economic security through marriage, and still others have never had an opportunity to work at all. This book, then, is close knit, woven by many women within a framework the authors built to embrace their accounts of successful aging.

WHAT FOLLOWS

In the chapters that follow, women with intellectual disabilities in 18 countries look back over their childhood experiences, family life, entry into adulthood, roles in society, the networks of economic and social supports available to them, and whether they have worked or otherwise contributed productively to their livelihood. They appraise their own health, well-being, and happiness. A cross-cultural approach presents the possibility of understanding the women's lives as exemplars of the history of system evolution in how their respective countries have identified and supported women with intellectual disabilities to date.

An overarching theme is that the women portrayed here are outsiders. They are removed from any normative benchmarks of human development and life in their own societies. Many have lately found new lives in ordinary homes in the community, but they spent their formative years and young adulthood in special, often separate, settings such as special residences. Although some have borne children, this life event has not always led to reciprocity of care nor to enduring parent–child bonds.

A second theme is the search for resilience, a human quality developed through many decades of living and arguably a mark of accomplishment, rather than of merely survival (see Chapter 2). Rowe and Kahn (1998) identified three components of successful aging for the general population: to stay free of disease or disability, to maintain functional skills, and to be engaged with life. Older people with intellectual disabilities may require particular support throughout their adult years to encounter each of these human experiences appropriately (Janicki & Ansello, 2000). The women in this study showed surprising resilience even in the teeth of unsatisfactory living arrangements not of their choosing (see Chapter 3), the loss of loved ones through separation or death (see Chapter 6), and insidious poverty and marginal livelihoods (see Chapter 4). They were, in the main, healthy (see Chapter 5), and their memories, worries, and dreams resembled those of other adults (see Chapter 7).

At the heart of the book lie the substantive findings of interviews carried out between research collaborators and the women themselves. These findings are presented in four thematic chapters with a common structure: Chapter 4, "Economic and Personal Safety Nets"; Chapter 5, "Health"; Chapter 6, "Social Roles"; and Chapter 7, "A Sense of Well-Being." Each comprises a brief literature review of published evidence relevant to that chapter's domain, a description of the quantitative and qualitative indicators applied, the findings of the interviews with the women, and a short discussion outlining directions for future research. The women's voices are threaded through each of these chapters.

Finally, the book is handwork made up of pieces drawn from many sources. The women who contributed do not know each other. Thus, we have sifted and shaped, discerning relationships and developing themes. We have made every effort to attend to what the women believe to have been important in their lives and to stitch these slips of fabric together to make a whole. The resulting texture of the book will surprise, delight, or perhaps even dismay its readers. We hope that it will also engage and provoke.

CHAPTER TWO

Successful Aging

An International Perspective

> She is a shrewd, intelligent, sensible
> woman. Hers is a line for seeing human nature;
> and she has a fund of good sense and observation
> which, as a companion, make her infinitely superior
> to thousands of those who having only received "the
> best education in the world," know nothing worth attending to.
>
> JANE AUSTEN, PERSUASION

This chapter presents the core themes and terms used in this book. First, it defines the population of women represented here. Next, it reviews briefly the literature related to the experiences of women with disabilities in their search for healthy, successful aging as they help to direct the course of their lives. Important issues related to completing cross-cultural research on gender, health, and aging are discussed critically. Global issues reflected in current policies related to gender, health, and disability are presented.

INTRODUCTION

Increased life expectancy will continue to generate a growing cohort of members of the third age (i.e., the life stage of active retirement) in every country, rich and poor alike. Women with intellectual disabilities who have already grown older successfully are a unique primary source of evidence and inspiration for today's younger women and girls. Their voices may authoritatively guide others engaged in a process of discovery leading to a good and healthy old age. But who are older women with intellectual disabilities, and where do they live?

Women who were born before 1960 are represented in this book for two reasons. First, there is evidence to suggest that some women with intellectual disabilities may age before their time: Their aging is precocious, and thus they may experience certain age-related biological changes before their peers. Second, although the population of people with intellectual disabilities living in developing countries is increasing rapidly, few have to date lived into their seventh decade, years when people in industrialized countries reach the third age. Women in this group have an important message: If policy makers and service providers know the correlates of healthy aging, they can start to create systems and communities where these features can flourish and become more available.

GENDER AND HEALTH

People of higher socioeconomic status in the industrialized world tend to have better health than their less prosperous peers. It seems likely that gender differences play a part, too, although the resulting inequalities vary according to life stage and health measures (Matthews, Manor, & Power, 1999). For example, large birth cohort studies indicate that unemployment contributes more to inequality for men and that for women family structure is important. In this way, gender is a determinant of health. Personal characteristics and gender interact with elements of the social, economic, physical, and political environments and help to determine the health status of individuals. Are these population patterns replicated in the lives of people with intellectual disabilities, a group distinguished in most countries by relative poverty, lack of education, pervasive unemployment, and social disadvantage?

HEALTHY AGING

Gender helps to determine health throughout the adult life course. For women with intellectual disabilities, longer life also brings greater exposure to age-related health risks for breast cancer and other illnesses typical for mature women. Other health conditions mirror those tending to arise in the general population of middle-age women: heart disease, thyroid problems, sensory impairments, and musculoskeletal disorders (van Schrojenstein Lantman-de Valk, 1998). However, these conditions tend to occur earlier among women with intellectual disabilities and are less likely to be treated until they reach a critical point. By contrast, it is possible that sexual inactivity among these women may diminish risks for cervical cancer. Communication difficulties, insensitive attitudes, untrained health professionals, and inaccessible medical procedures are additional sources of disadvantage as women try to achieve healthy aging (Walsh & Heller, 2002).

Women in mid-life are also vulnerable to depression, anxiety, and adjustment disorders, conditions more prevalent among people with intellectual and other developmental disabilities than within the general population (Stavrakaki, 1999). A woman in her forties or fifties may suffer the loss of a parent but manifest signs of depression belatedly. Those with more severe levels of intellectual disability or communication difficulties may express lowered mood through behaviors such as aggression, sleep disturbance, or lethargy. Adults who have lived in settings of deprivation may have poorer health and fewer resources to cope with abrupt life changes or other stresses (Thorpe, Davidson, & Janicki, 2001). Older women with intellectual disabilities may also bear the impact of lifelong medication regimens. Many have lived in institutions since childhood and have experienced years of poor diet and low levels of physical activity. Most have limited educational attainments and are thus poorly equipped to adjust to complex environments demanding high levels of literacy.

As is common with their peers, people with intellectual disabilities enjoy an increasing life expectancy: those with an etiology other than Down syndrome will reach their sixties and beyond (World Health Organization, 2000). As they grow older, men and women require supports for living and working matched to their changing needs and vulnerability to age-related diseases such as dementia. In later life, they are at greater risk for developing the diseases associated with aging such as cardiovascular disease. Postmenopausal women have a heightened risk of developing weaker, more porous bones and a greater risk of fracture.

AGING IN CONTEXT

Health gain means increasing life expectancy, improving health during life, and minimizing disability. It means that people are equipped and supported so that they may adjust to their environments, prosper, and make contributions to the lives of others. It is a lifelong pursuit, rather than a one-time endowment. At the extreme end of the life cycle, the very old—those older than 85 years—are vulnerable to a host of age-related conditions. An allied goal for all citizens is social gain, achieved by adding quality to the lives of people who have disabilities or a long-term illness or who are vulnerable because of age or incapacity.

Political and economic constraints set obvious limits to key health indicators such as life expectancy: A Norwegian woman may expect to outlive her counterpart in India (United Nations Development Programme, 1999). As life expectancy increases, the quality of life among older people looms as a health target. Gender plays a part in reaching these targets among women in the general population. Robine, Romieu, and Cambois (1999) examined health expectancy calculations across 49 countries, mostly those with developed market economies. They observed that the proportion of morbidity-free years to life expectancy is slightly lower for women, possibly because of their longer survival after the development of a disability or handicap. No comparable data for women with intellectual or other lifelong disabilities are available.

Women do not always live as long as they might, relative to men. Social circumstances and cultural practices compromise the greater longevity they might otherwise expect. The link between gender and health reflects the complex influences of the social, economic, and cultural environments on women's lives at each stage of the lifespan. Their experiences of friendship, intimacy, family life, employment, leisure, and personal satisfaction both reflect their times and are tempered by cultural expectations. Social, economic, and political disadvantages are detrimental to women's health. Teasing out the influence of gender or the presence of intellectual disabilities in women's lives on their health is a complex task. Access to health and medical care is necessary, if not sufficient, for women with intellectual disabilities to enjoy equal opportunities for social inclusion, according to the United Nations' *Standard Rules for the Equalization of Opportunities for People with Disabilities* (1994).

Women have different health concerns and circumstances as they age. Arguably these are not yet fully understood for the general population of women, and certainly the factors associated with health among women with intellectual disabilities have only recently been explored. Although people with intellectual disabilities share the same health needs as the general population—including surveillance measures relevant to women's health—they have additional, special health needs. Yet adequate primary health services for this population remain an unmet target even in a relatively well-to-do country such as the United Kingdom (Kerr, 1998).

DETERMINING OUTCOMES

Self-determination is a key element in conceptualizing *quality of life,* a construct increasingly applied across cultures (Keith & Schalock, 2000). An ecological approach to self-determination encompasses personal control, self-determination competencies, and environmental influences. Consensus is growing that it is good practice to offer personalized, flexible supports to individuals in core areas of adult life (e.g., making choices about how to lead one's life and having a personal budget to implement these choices). Yet, adults with intellectual disabilities exercise fewer choices than men and women who do not have disabilities. Making personal choices in order to take some control over one's daily life and future plans is an important element within self-determination.

A core element in measures of quality of life is the degree to which the individual exercises autonomy about everyday decisions. Recent attempts to conceptualize and measure self-determination have helped to illuminate how individuals may be encouraged to make choices. This dispositional characteristic is expressed in self-regulation, psychological empowerment, self-realization, and autonomy, emerging as individuals become competent at directing their own lives (Wehmeyer, 1996).

Do women with intellectual disabilities experience particular hazards in determining the course of their own lives? This question has not yet been systematically addressed. If it proves to be true that women with intellectual disabilities lag in self-direction and autonomy in all aspects of their social and civic lives, it might be argued that they share with other women in their culture a stereotypic gender role. Arguably, such roles emerge from the productive work that men and women typically do. Gender and other social roles are linked to distinctive behaviors that may become stereotyped in cultures in which gender inequality holds sway and traditional male and female occupations diverge to reflect communal (feminine) versus agentic (masculine) behaviors (Eagly & Wood, 1999). Or it may be that both women and men with intellectual disabilities—as suggested by a compelling body of evidence—lack the opportunity to make choices for themselves (Stalker & Harris, 1998). Further research is needed to explore these distinct but related issues.

GLOBAL ISSUES

Globally, a gap exists between the wealthy, industrialized countries, where life is long, and the least developed countries, where life is short and often harsh.

Opportunities for good health and a good life may be separate and unequal even within countries. In countries where women—particularly those with intellectual disabilities—are not valued, their lesser status is reflected in limited access to health care, education, and employment. Individuals with intellectual disabilities require lifelong supports at home, in the workplace, and in the wider community in order to enhance their quality of life. Factors operating at every level in the environment help to determine the quality of life experienced by women with intellectual disabilities in each country. Economic prosperity makes it more likely that governments will extend entitlements to a range of health and social services. A society committed to solidarity and equity among all citizens favors social inclusion. Cultures express themselves in attitudes toward diversity, inclusion, and gender equality and in the meanings conferred on terms such as *group homes* or *family supports*. At the national level, political will is decisive in shaping and enforcing antidiscrimination laws.

Global policies have special resonance for women with intellectual disabilities. The United Nations' *Standard Rules for the Equalization of Opportunities for People with Disabilities* apply universally: Equal access to health and medical services is a core principle. Although without status in international law, these 22 rules exert a compelling moral force. The World Health Organization builds gender-sensitive approaches to health care delivery and to the promotion of women's health by ensuring that it takes part in planning and monitoring interventions, by making health systems more responsive to women's needs, and by enacting policies to promote gender equality. In every country, most of the unpaid work of caring for a family member who depends on others for her or his livelihood takes its toll in terms of economic opportunities lost on the part of mothers, sisters, and grandmothers (United Nations Development Programme, 1999). Addressing the needs of family caregivers, most of whom are women, is a critical path to supporting people with disabilities optimally.

Today's older women with intellectual disabilities live in a territory where political will, social change, and economic status intersect, where history washes up against sea changes in policy, where private accomplishments meet public perceptions, and where individuals shape lives within their own cultures. Understanding how each has succeeded in attaining a good age is authentic testimony for the next generation of women.

CROSS-CULTURAL PERSPECTIVES

Women from minority groups are more likely to have intellectual disabilities than their majority counterparts. They are also more likely to be viewed negatively by the dominant culture and therefore are less likely than women with disabilities from the dominant culture to have opportunities for community living, employment, independence, and healthy outcomes. In the United States, fewer than 20% of these women are employed. Few of these women live independently or have many social activities or relationships outside of the home. Few of these women receive routine health maintenance screens or interventions for diseases until the disease has progressed to a late stage. And yet, many of these women live healthy, fulfilling lives outside of usual expectations or opportunities.

These same women, in another culture or setting, may experience an entirely different belief system and therefore alternative expectations. Individuals and nations with diverse ethnic and cultural backgrounds have different perceptions regarding disability, illness, disease, help-seeking behavior, and self-determination. It is important to recognize that each of these terms is defined by the culture in which it is used. According to Taylor (1997), five possible areas of influence shape an individual's perceptions of disability, including

1. *Historical discrimination:* Racism and stereotyping by the dominant culture has resulted in minority group members seeking alternative definitions and service systems.

2. *Religion:* For many cultures, perceptions of disability are centered in religious beliefs. For some cultures, disability is a blessing from God; for others, it is a punishment.

3. *Malevolent forces:* Some cultures believe disability is the result of spirits, entities, or forces in the universe.

4. *Superstition:* Some cultures believe disability occurs due to some action on the part of a person or the person's family.

5. *Socioeconomic status:* The higher a minority member's socioeconomic status is, the more likely that person's perceptions about disability will mirror the perception of the dominant culture.

In conducting cross-cultural research, it is important to understand how individuals, families, and communities view women, disability, illness, and help-seeking. This study attempts to define *gender, disability, health,* and *aging* within the context of the system in which the women in this book must live. That context becomes defined by the beliefs, interpersonal styles, attitudes, language, and behaviors of individuals within the culture. Individuals may live within a subculture of a dominant culture (e.g., a Latino community in the United States) or within a nation whose culture is ethnically and culturally different from a Euro-American–centered model (e.g., Japan). Our intent is to paint a multicolored collage of women with intellectual disabilities who are aging successfully.

Variation in how women with intellectual disabilities find support is very great. National governments in many poorer, less developed countries may not fund formal systems. Countries with more developed economies may vary in the extent to which they have established legal underpinning for systems of entitlement and other supports. Issues of access within systems in developed countries persist, so that women and other less valued groups encounter barriers. Subtle differences in the thrust of social policy are apparent even within a region such as the Nordic countries of Europe (Tøssebro, Gustavsson, & Dyrendahl, 1996).

Old age is more visible in more wealthy countries of the developed world, where 12.6% of the population is elderly, than in developing countries, where only 4.6% are elderly (World Health Organization, 1998). In developing countries, ordinary employment may be elusive, notwithstanding the pressures on women and men with intellectual disabilities to contribute to their family's livelihood. Those who find work are likely to do so in traditional agriculture, production, or other forms of self-employment. In many developing countries, thousands of people with disabilities and their families have scant opportunity to earn enough income to support themselves with even basic daily requirements.

SUMMARY

What is successful aging? The search for a consensus unifying women across cultures is a core theme of this book. How do women make choices at different stages of their lives? What sources of support do they prize? How do they appraise their accomplishments in growing older? To discover the path to successful aging, women with intellectual disabilities who are growing older wisely and well around the world were invited to respond to these questions. In the next chapter, the research methodology used in collecting information about the health and social systems of many countries and in documenting the stories told by women themselves is presented.

CHAPTER THREE

Collecting Information and Stories

In April 1999, researchers in the field of aging and intellectual disabilities met at a special roundtable on healthy aging at the headquarters of the World Health Organization in Geneva, Switzerland. One subgroup of that roundtable was charged with the task of developing a working paper on the health of women with intellectual disabilities. Following 2 days of intense and wide-ranging discussions, a key discovery began to emerge from the participants: We did not have a good picture of normative aging for women with intellectual disabilities. What we knew from the literature was based on a medical model, focused on a disease and deterioration orientation to aging. We began to challenge that orientation on the basis of our own individual and personal experiences and relationships with older women with intellectual disabilities. We did not want to build a policy, service, and support model based on a reductionary, disease orientation to aging. The idea of painting the picture within the picture began to resonate with the participants. Questions began to emerge within the group: Who are older women with intellectual disabilities? Are they different depending where they live in the world? What are their life experiences? Is aging introducing new opportunities? Do they have a story to share with young women with intellectual disabilities? What could and should we learn from their lives? After the euphoria that always accompanies brainstorming and the brief opening of new windows on discovery, we began to identify all of the methodological and practical barriers to gathering these women's stories, an activity that was particularly necessary if we wanted to capture these stories across multiple countries and cultures. We left the roundtable with little further practical discussion about how to develop a normative baseline. However, the desire to discover and tell these women's stories did not disappear. At professional meetings, we continued to float the idea, and it continued to resonate. We received encouraging and varied correspondence related to this project idea. Many colleagues expressed strong enthusiasm and willingness to gather stories in their communities. And so, this descriptive, highly qualitative project on successful aging for women with intellectual disabilities was launched.

This chapter presents the study methodology used in collecting data for this book. First, it describes the genesis of the study concept. Next, the study design—including study questions, protocol, collaborator and participant recruitment, and interview procedures—are described, followed by the data analysis strategy. Third, the national and cultural contexts for the stories are described. Fourth, the chapter concludes with a description of the study participants. Finally, the limitations of the study design are discussed, particularly in light of interview challenges and issues of generalization.

STUDY DESIGN

Several steps went into the design of this study. We identified major questions in order to fix a direction for the study. A protocol was established so that the identified questions could be answered in a fairly consistent manner. Collaborators and study participants from around the world were recruited. Finally, we made decisions about interview procedures and data analysis.

Major Questions

The questions addressed in this study can be organized into five dimensions:

1. *Demographics:* Who are these women? What is the nature of their interpersonal relationships? Do they have children? Where do they live? What is their education history? What is their work history?

2. *Economic and personal safety nets:* What is the nature of their economic and personal supports?

3. *Health:* How do these women perceive their personal health? What is the nature of their health care? Do they have healthy lifestyles?

4. *Social roles:* What is the nature of their relationships and roles with their families and friends? Have those relationships and roles changed? How do these women spend their days?

5. *Well-being:* How do these women perceive the quality of their lives? What do they dream and worry about? What insights do they have for young girls with intellectual disabilities?

The overarching framework for addressing these questions is grounded in ecological systems theory. This theory places the individual within her familial, organizational, and social structural contexts. The framework acknowledges the interdependence among the various elements and contexts, the fluidity of that interdependence over time, and the influence of social, political, and governmental philosophies and policies on it.

Protocol

The interview protocol consisted of 102 questions, divided into five sections, that addressed the five broad question areas. The demographics section contained 19 questions that addressed the woman's age, racial/ethnic background, marital status, type of disability, place of residence, childbirth experience, living arrangement and co-inhabitants, educational experience, and work experience. The second section on economic and personal safety nets contained 15 questions that addressed the woman's support providers and their relationships to her; the level, types, and reliability of the support provided; her sources of economic support and her control of finances; and her participation and independence in activities of daily living (ADLs). The next section on health included 18 questions that addressed the woman's perceptions of her health, her access to and use of routine health care, medications, secondary health concerns, and health maintenance and healthy lifestyle activities. The fourth section on social roles included 21 items addressing family relationships, friendships, informal and formal support networks, and leisure activities. The fifth and last section of the interview addressed well-being. It contained 29 items that explored the woman's perceptions of various aspects of quality-of-life issues, decision making, coping strategies, daily routines, dreams, worries, future aspirations, and personal reflections. Overall, the protocol presented the interview queries in a mix of formats, including close-ended, open-ended, multiple-choice, and graphic questions. The complete interview protocol is presented in the appendix.

Recruitment of Collaborators

Potential collaborators from other countries were identified from three primary sources: those disability researchers who participated in the World Health Organization's 1999 roundtable, colleagues of the authors from previous work on disability issues, and colleagues from professional associations and networks whom we knew were interested in women with intellectual disabilities. Our goal was to gather at least 10 stories from 20 distinct countries, for a total of 200 stories. A packet of information was sent to the potential collaborators that contained a cover letter describing the study, a commitment form, guidelines for collaboration and data collection, a schedule, a brief questionnaire to obtain a profile of their country's disability statistics and services, and the interview protocol. Thirty information packets were disseminated and 21 colleagues returned commitment forms, representing 18 countries. Upon receipt of the completed interviews, each collaborator was paid an honorarium.

Recruitment of Study Participants

Collaborators in each country were asked to recruit 10 older women with intellectual disabilities to participate in the interviews. Collaborators were free to recruit the women by methods that they typically used in their other research studies, such as through personal contacts with disability service providers, advocacy organizations, and women with intellectual disabilities; presentations at professional conferences; articles and advertisements in disability newsletters; flyers; and word of mouth. Only women who were older than 40 and had an intellectual disability were eligible to participate in the study. In addition to confirming prior to the interview that the woman met the two criteria, each collaborator also determined each participant's eligibility through record verification or her case manager or service provider. Each participant was provided with full written and oral information about the study's aims and plans for ensuing publications, and she was given guarantees of confidentiality and anonymity, following the guidelines of the institutional review boards of the study authors' and the collaborators' research institutions. Signed consent to participate was secured from each participant. Compensation for the participants was addressed on a per country basis, with some collaborators paying a monetary stipend to the women for their participation.

Interview Procedure

Prior to full-scale implementation of the protocol across the participating countries, the instrument was field-tested with women with a range of communication, intellectual, and interpersonal characteristics. Following feedback from the interviewers in the field test, adjustments were made to the format and length of the protocol. In order to implement the interviews in non-English–speaking countries, each collaborator translated the protocol into the native language of the participant prior to conducting the interview. The interview was subsequently conducted and recorded in the participant's native language and then translated back into English by the collaborator for data entry and interpretation.

Interviews were conducted face to face, in a place and time chosen by the participant. The majority of interviews were conducted at the site of the women's day activity programs, and a few interviews were conducted in women's homes. The interviews were conducted in privacy, with only the interviewer and interviewee present in the vast majority of situations. Each interview took 2–3 hours to conduct, depending on the dyad's rapport and the amount of information that was forthcoming. Participant fatigue did not appear to be a problem, as the majority of women expressed enthusiasm and happiness in being able to relate their stories.

Data Analysis

A mixture of quantitative and qualitative methods of data analysis was undertaken, including careful descriptions of each variable and inductive analyses of relationships and trends within the data. Many collaborators provided augmentative notes for their interviews, and as much as possible, informal interviews were held with each collaborator following the completion of all interviews to gather their qualitative reflections on the experience and their insights about the interview content and the participants.

Quantifiable data such as age, living arrangements, and family supports were categorized and entered into a relational database. Analyses included descriptive statistics, as well as inferential statistics to examine differences by age cohorts, geographic regions, and several personal attributes (living arrangement, primary support structure, and most important personal relationship). For purposes of analysis, the age range of the study participants was divided into three age cohorts: 40–55 years (i.e., middle age), 56–70 years (i.e., young old), and 71 years and older (the oldest). Geographic regions were divided into five categories: North America (Canada and the United States); Europe (Austria, Belgium, England, Finland, France, Ireland, Italy, Northern Ireland, Norway, and Scotland); South America (Argentina and Brazil); Asia (Japan and Taiwan); and Oceania (Australia and New Zealand). Living arrangement was categorized as family home, independent home (in a house or apartment), group home, or institution. Primary support structure was characterized as formal (paid support), informal (unpaid, voluntary support), or mixed (a combination of formal and informal support). Most important personal relationship was categorized as family member, care provider, or friend. The influence of various personal attributes on specific study questions was examined based on the literature supports for the possible existence of such influences. These questions by influence relationships are further discussed in each ensuing chapter.

STUDY COUNTRIES

As presented in Table 1, collaborators from 18 countries participated in this study, representing Europe, the Americas, Asia, and Oceania. Although these countries vary widely in terms of population size, the majority of the countries are strikingly similar in overall population variables. Two indicators that have a degree of variance include the percentage of population older than 65 and the index of human development and therefore quality-of-life ranking. With regard to aging in the population, both Brazil and Taiwan have relatively young populations (<10% older than 65) as compared with the other countries. For the human development index and the quality-of-life ranking, figures were taken from the *Pocket World in Figures* (2002), which is published by

Table 1.   Study countries

Region	Countries	Number of participants
Europe	Austria	10
	Belgium	10
	England	10
	Finland	3
	France	10
	Ireland	4
	Italy	10
	Northern Ireland	5
	Norway	10
	Scotland	10
North America	Canada	9
	United States	21
South America	Argentina	10
	Brazil	7
Asia	Japan	10
	Taiwan	10
Oceania	Australia	8
	New Zealand	10

The Economist. As defined by the United Nations Development Programme, the human development index is a combination of average years of schooling, adult literacy, life expectancy, and income levels. The index is scaled from 0 to 100. A score of 80 or above indicates that a country has a high human development level. A score of 50–79 indicates a medium human development level, and a score below 50 is considered low. The quality-of-life ranking is based on the country's human development score, comparing 80 countries throughout the world (*The Economist,* 2002, p. 28). With regard to human development, the South American countries have the lowest ratings among the study countries, with resultant global rankings for overall quality of life of 35 for Argentina and 68 for Brazil. However, compared with the rest of the world, Argentina has a high human development score (83.7), and Brazil has a medium human development score (74.7). Table 2 presents the series of national indicators and quality-of-life rank for each available study country. No data on national indicators were available on Scotland and Northern Ireland, and only limited data were available on Taiwan.

Disability Statistics by Region and Study Countries

Table 2 also includes the disability population statistics by region and study country. Where statistics are available, we present information on the percentage of people within each country who have disabilities. The way in which countries define *disability* for purposes of statistics gathering varies widely, with some countries only including more moderate and severe forms of intellectual, physical, and sensory disabilities, while other countries include a much broader range of a larger number of disabilities. We asked the collaborators from the participating countries to provide data on the prevalence of intellectual disabilities among people with disabilities and specifically among older people with disabilities. The majority of collaborators indicated it was difficult or impossible to provide this data due to the lack of reliable national statistics. Therefore, we can only report that the prevalence of people with intellectual disabilities across countries was reported to range from 1% to 12% of the population. The percentage of people with intellectual disabilities who were older than 50 was reported to range from 8% to 26% of the total intellectual disability population.

Characteristics of the Disability Service System by Country

With the exception of Brazil, all of the study countries had some provision for financial support and services for adults with intellectual disabilities. Brazil reported very few services for people with intellectual disabilities, and the

Table 2. National indicators

Region/country	Population (in millions)	% with a disability	% older than 65	Life expectancy for men	Life expectancy for women	Human development score	Quality-of-life rank
Europe							
Austria	8.1	—	20.7	75.4	81.5	90.8	16
Belgium	10.2	9.0	22.1	75.7	81.9	92.5	7
Finland	5.1	—	19.9	74.4	81.5	91.7	11*
France	60.8	10.0	20.5	75.2	82.8	91.7	11*
Ireland	3.7	—	15.2	74.4	79.6	90.7	18
Italy	57.4	—	24.1	75.5	81.9	90.3	19*
Northern Ireland	—	—	—	—	—	—	—
Norway	4.5	36.0	19.6	76.0	81.9	93.4	2
Scotland	—	20.0	—	—	—	—	—
United Kingdom	59.1	12.0	20.6	75.7	80.7	91.8	10
North America							
Canada	30.6	15.5	16.7	76.2	81.8	93.5	1
United States	272.9	19.7	16.1	74.6	80.4	92.9	3*
South America							
Argentina	36.3	—	13.3	70.6	77.7	83.7	35
Brazil	168.0	—	7.8	64.7	72.6	74.7	68
Asia							
Japan	126.5	—	23.2	77.8	85.0	92.4	9
Taiwan	21.9	3.7	8.3	—	—	—	—
Oceania							
Australia	19.0	18.0	16.3	76.4	82.0	92.9	3*
New Zealand	3.8	19.6	15.6	75.3	80.7	90.3	19*

* Denotes countries that are tied in rankings for quality of life

services that did exist were of low quality. In the other study countries, the services were provided most often through a combination of government-supported (i.e., public) programs and programs operated by voluntary organizations. Services included housing, day activity and sheltered workshops, community employment, and a few senior citizen programs.

Study Participants

As illustrated in Table 1, 167 women from five geographic regions made up of 18 countries participated in this study. Although it was determined prior to each interview that each participant did, indeed, have an intellectual disability, each woman was asked to describe her disability. They each acknowledged in their own terms that they had intellectual disabilities; however, their identification of that characteristic tended to be expressed in more functional terms, rather than in medical or psychological terminology. For example, many women gave such responses as, "I am a bit slower than other people," "I have trouble reading and learning," and "I need help buying clothes and organizing things." Table 3 describes the demographic characteristics of the women, including their age, ethnicity, formal schooling, and marital status

Table 3. Participant characteristics

Characteristic	Number	Percentage
Age cohorts (n = 157)		
40–55 years	70	44.6
56–70 years	69	43.9
71+ years	18	11.5
Race/ethnicity (n = 157)		
Asian	22	14.0
Caucasian/European	126	80.3
Aboriginal/Native	9	5.7
Formal education (yes)	116	73.9
Type of school (n = 116)		
Primary	23	20.0
Secondary	22	19.1
Special school	71	60.9
Marital status (single)	137	87.2
Children (yes)	30	19.4
North America	4	13.3
Europe	14	20.0
South America	2	11.8
Asia	8	40.0
Oceania	2	11.1

and whether they had children. The mean age of the study participants was 57 years, with a range of 40–82 years. With regard to race, nine aboriginal/indigenous participants came from Argentina, Brazil, Australia, and New Zealand. Across the three age cohorts, equal percentages of women reported that they had received some formal education. Asian women were the least likely to report that they had received some formal education (69%), while women living in the Oceanic region were most likely to report some formal education (89%). Although the majority of women were single, seven of the 18 countries in the study contained at least one woman who reported that she was currently married (n = 20). Overall, 26 women (16.5%) reported either current or past significant relationships with men (e.g., living with a man, widowed, divorced). The percentage of women who had children were distributed equally across the three age cohorts. Thirty women from 12 of the 18 countries reported that they had children. By percentage, Asian women were the most likely to have children, while Oceanic women were the least likely to have children. The 30 mothers had a total of 70 children, with up to 6 children per mother. Table 4 describes the number of women with children by age cohorts and geographic regions.

Limitations of the Study

This study cannot be characterized as a scientific research study, nor was it intended to be one. It is best envisioned as a quilt—a multicolored, multilayered cloth that was lived by women, gathered by women (largely), and pieced together by us to present an image where there had not been one before. Could

Table 4.   Women in the study who have children, categorized by participant's age cohort and geographic region (n = 70)

Demographic grouping	Number	Percentage
Age cohorts		
40–55 years	29	41.4
56–70 years	32	45.7
71+ years	9	12.9
Geographic regions		
North America	8	11.4
Europe	27	38.6
South America*	7	10.0
Asia*	26	37.1
Oceania	2	2.9

*All of the South American children were born to women in Argentina; all of the Asian children were born to women in Taiwan.

the stories have been stitched together in a way other than that which we have chosen? Of course. However, we have attempted to capture a story from these pieces of cloth, in an attempt to stimulate more scientific directions and questions for future research related to aging, women, and intellectual disabilities. Because these stories are from a convenience sample of women, the experiences of these women cannot be generalized to all older women with intellectual disabilities. We do not intend for such a generalization nor do we encourage it. We want to illuminate patterns in the material, themes that seem to weave in and out, to highlight some of the unique colors and to emphasize the common threads that seem to run across all of the stories, independent of countries, cultures, and service systems. Most important, and sadly for us, we are limited by not having been able to sit in on every interview and hear the hesitations in certain responses, the joy in others, the ease and the struggle in coming to new understandings simply by focusing on a particular question. That crucial limitation sometimes diminishes our ability to portray the richness of these women's lives, but we hope that this book will encourage you to seek personal experience in order to recognize the uniqueness of each woman with an intellectual disability and the commonality of each woman with all women who are living into their third age.

CHAPTER FOUR

Economic and Personal Safety Nets

We depend on everyone; no one wants us.
We are penny ante—penny ante jobs, penny ante lives.
An older woman who works in a sheltered workshop

Gloria came into the interview in a large electric wheelchair, laden with three bags of miscellaneous items, her water bottle, and her purse. She wore a dress, shoes with socks, and a heavy winter coat. She insisted that she wanted to keep her coat on, although she perspired heavily throughout the interview. She finally agreed to remove her coat when a care worker who came in to empty her urine bag reprimanded Gloria for making the room smell from her perspiration. Gloria laughed and said she would try better next time. She winked at the interviewer. Gloria is 60 years old, and she has cerebral palsy, mild intellectual disability, and (by self-report) a history of depression. Although she used to walk with some difficulty, she has "given in to the wheelchair" in the past few years. In addition to her limited mobility, Gloria has glaucoma and diabetes. She seems anxious about the interview, and it becomes quite clear that she wants her story to "go well." She says she wants to tell about a "happy life."

Gloria lived at home with her parents, two sisters, and one brother until she was 13 years old. She says, "I was happy as a lark, and then the problems came out and I was sent to an institution." She lived in the institution for 10 years, and then she moved to a group home. She has been living in her current group home for 4 years. She has four female housemates, and the home is owned and operated by a husband and wife, Ken and Susan. Ken and Susan handle all of Gloria's finances. She says, "They are good people but sometimes a bit cranky." Staff handle the operation of the home and help Gloria with her personal care. She impishly says she could help with making meals, but she lets them take care of it. "Sometimes, I get into fights with my care provider and then they don't come back. I have stopped trying to learn their names. They keep changing all the time." Yet, Gloria is quick to say that her care providers are her primary supports. They have helped her through rough times—depression, loss of mobility, death of family members. All and all, Gloria puts a face of optimism on her situation by saying, "Sometimes people just don't want to work with us [people with disabilities]. You gotta have a heart to do this work."

Gloria has only occasional contact with her family, although she could tell the names and addresses of her sister and brother and their children. Both of her parents and one of her sisters have died. Her other sister "comes when she can get there." Her sister manages a trust fund that Gloria's father left for her. Last year, she gave Gloria some money to buy a new wheelchair. Gloria thought for a while about her family and their visits and she said, "Maybe I will see my niece at Easter," although it sounded more like a wish than a fact. The most striking thing she wanted us to know about her brother is that he lives 2,000 miles away.

Gloria says she attended high school, although it is unclear what this meant in the context of an institutional setting. She says she works as she wishes in a sheltered workshop. She can't recall if she ever had any other type of job. She does light parts assembly tasks for a penny per part. But she quickly adds, "There's no work right now, so we sit a lot." The money she makes goes into a workshop fund that the staff use to hold parties and outings for the workers. Gloria says she wishes she had some money to buy clothes and personal items. "I think I would be happier if I had money."

Gloria lights up when she mentions Tom, "the love of my life." Gloria said she fell in love with Tom in grade school, but "he had a bad heart and we can't see each other." (Tom apparently also has a disability and has recently had bypass surgeries.) They talk to each other on the telephone but don't see each other anymore. Gloria still dreams that she might live in the same house with Tom one day. She says, "Maybe I'll ask my case worker."

Hours run into days, days into months, and months into years for Gloria. She says her routines are the same: "Up at 5:10 A.M., do some therapeutic exercises, dress, wait for a van to the sheltered workshop, work if I want, [at] 2:30 go home, watch TV or listen to the radio, have dinner at 5:30, have a bath, and go to bed at 8:30." Monday and Saturday are the same as any weekday. "Maybe on Sunday, someone will take me to church. I am Methodist, but I'll go to any church." Gloria can't remember the last time that "someone came." When we ask if she goes to movies, restaurants, parks, or the shopping mall, she answers each item the same, "Once in a while, if staff want to do something to get out of the house. We all pile in the van and go." Gloria can't remember ever going on a vacation. Once she went to a "cp [cerebral palsy] camp and it cost [my] family $400."

Gloria says she worries about her health and being alone with no one to care for her. Sometimes she wants to stay in bed all day. But, she insists she is very happy, repeating, "I am not sad, I am not sad." When asked to speculate about what her life will be like 5 years from now, Gloria says, "I will have my own apartment, with a roommate who can walk and talk—maybe it will be Tom, if his heart can take it." Her care provider knocks on the door to say, "Come for lunch now or miss it today." Gloria winks at the interviewer, turns on the power button on her wheelchair, and says, "We were just finished."

Women with intellectual disabilities depend on external economic and personal safety nets for their subsistence. This chapter presents a review of the current literature on personal economics and support systems for people with disabilities. Following the review, findings from our study are presented, including a description of the economic and personal safety nets in these women's lives and how those nets differ by age, living arrangements, and geographic regions of the world. The chapter concludes with a discussion of the similarities and differences between the older women with intellectual disabilities in our study and the findings in the current literature.

DISABILITY, INCOME, AND ECONOMIC SAFETY NET

As a demographic group, people with disabilities are poor. In a 2002 editorial, Wolfensohn, the president of the World Bank, put the issue in a global perspective: Of the 1.3 billion people who live in extreme poverty worldwide, the majority of the world's 400 million people with disabilities "live at the bottom of the pile." In a landmark article on the changing universe of disability, Seelman and Sweeney indicated that "poverty is the primary screening indicator of the many variables that increase the risk of disability" (1995, p. 2). From a sociological perspective, Slee emphasized that the relationship between disability and poverty is axiomatic, given "the complex interaction of material (political economy) and nonmaterial (biological) factors that conspire to disable people in real social and historical contexts" (1996, pp. 98–99). He indicated that there is a growing mass of international statistical data that demonstrates the materially precarious position of people with disabilities

(p. 99). In fact, a study by British researchers conservatively estimated that half of all people with disabilities in the United Kingdom are living in poverty (Berthoud, Lakey, & McKay, 1993).

In the United States, results of an analysis of the U.S. National Health Interview Survey, Disability Supplement (NHIS-D), indicated that approximately 36.1% of noninstitutionalized Americans with an intellectual and/or developmental disability live in households with incomes below the poverty level, compared with 12.9% of all households (Larson, Larkin, Anderson, & Kwak, 2001). Further analysis indicated that, among all people with intellectual and/or developmental disabilities, gender, educational attainment, and living arrangement affected economic status. Specifically, women were 1.34 times more likely to live in poverty than men, individuals with no education were 5.7 times more likely to live in poverty, and people living alone or with a non-relative were 1.43 times more likely to live in poverty (Larson et al., 2001).

Historically, researchers and disability theorists have contended that disability, in and of itself, destined individuals with disabilities to lives that were earmarked by a compromised quality of life and low economic status. Certainly due to poor educational opportunities, low employment rates, and ongoing health needs, the lives of people with disabilities are, economically speaking, less than optimal. However, emerging research is uncovering the more complex relationship between poverty and disability. Rather than a simple linear relationship between the two variables—which would imply that if a person has a disability, then he or she will be poor—current literature recognizes the interactional relationship between disability and poverty. The cumulative and negative effects of poverty and disability are being identified in the literature as sociological double jeopardy.

Several authors have specifically studied the existence and impact of this double jeopardy. Fujiura and Yamaki (1997, 2000) used U.S. national databases to examine the covariation of poverty and disability. In their 1997 study, using data from the U.S. Census Bureau's Survey of Income and Program Participation (SIPP), they found that households with a family member with developmental disabilities had significantly lower income and greater dependence on means-tested income support than typical families. In the 2000 study, using data from the U.S. National Health Interview Survey (NHIS), they found an increased risk for disability among constituencies defined by poverty and single-parent families. Specifically, they found that disability prevalence remained flat over a 14-year period for children at or above the poverty line, but rates for children below the poverty line increased from 7.8% to 11.1%. Newacheck and Halfon (1998) also used the NHIS and they found that prevalence of disability was higher for children from low-income families. Laplante and Carlson (1996) and Sherman (1994) found an increased likelihood for intellectual disabilities and special education participation among children living in poverty. McNeil (1997) found in an analysis of the SIPP that 42% of Americans with disabilities were living in poverty, compared with 13% of the general population.

In a series of studies on the welfare population in the United States, the relationship between poverty and disability is evident. Lee, Sills, and Oh (2002) at the Institute for Women's Policy Research found that single mothers receiving welfare were more likely to have a child with a disability than other mothers with low incomes (20% and 11%, respectively). In addition, they found that the mothers receiving welfare themselves were more likely to have a disability than other mothers who have low incomes (38% and 17%, respectively). Specifically, they found that nearly half of single mothers receiving welfare have a disability or a child with a disability, but only a small proportion receives government supports. Similarly, Sweeney (2001, 2002) found that 40% of women receiving welfare had a disability so severe as to limit their ability to work. She also found that up to half of the women who were sanctioned for not seeking work had disabilities that interfered with their ability to work.

Park, Turnbull, and Turnbull (2002) examined the impact of poverty on family quality of life. They suggested that 28% of children with disabilities are living in poor families, a fact that has negative effects on five dimensions of family life: health (e.g., hunger, limited care), productivity (e.g., delayed cognitive development), environment (e.g., overcrowded home, unsafe neighborhood), emotional well-being (e.g., stress, low self-esteem), and family interaction (e.g., marital conflict, inconsistent parenting). These findings were corroborated by a Michigan study that found that family poverty translated into delayed and low-quality medical and dental care, greater possibility for children's going to bed hungry, few options for external care supports, lack of transportation options, and stressed and depressed caregivers (Zehnder-Merrell, 2001).

In ongoing research at the Organisation for Economic Co-operation and Development (OECD), disability prevalence, poverty, and resource allocation for students receiving special education is being examined across the 37-member constituency. An initial study found that disability prevalence rates were increasing for children living in poverty across all OECD member countries (LeRoy, Evans, & DeLuca, 2000). For example, in Ireland, overall childhood disability prevalence rates were increasing, and in particular, higher rates of disability prevalence were observed in areas of the country that also had high rates of socioeconomic disadvantage. Italy reported similar disparities related to geographic areas of the country and their socioeconomic conditions. Even in countries in which population-based rates of disability and family poverty are low (e.g., Scandinavian countries), research indicates that disability still appears to be differentiated by economic status (Sonnander & Claesson, 1999). In a second OECD-initiated study that examined the relationship between poverty and disability among students receiving special education, a correlation that ranged between .68 and .83 was found across several Michigan school districts (LeRoy & Kulik, 2002).

A few studies have specifically examined economic indicators for women with disabilities. In an analysis of the U.S. Census Bureau data, Szalda-Petree, Seekins, and Innis (1999) found that poverty is severe for women with disabilities. In particular, they found that urban women with disabilities are seven times more likely and rural women with disabilities are eight times more likely to earn less than $10,000 per year, as compared with people without disabilities. Less than 10% of the remaining women with disabilities, across both urban and rural settings, earned more than $20,000. In examining income by gender, residence, and age, they found that more than 70% of women with disabilities older than 65 years earned less than $10,000 per year. Again, older women with disabilities experienced the highest rate of severe poverty. Crewe and Clarke (1996), in a study of women with physical disabilities, listed poverty as a significant and pervasive stressor in their lives.

Sources of Income for People with Disabilities

According to a Harris Interactive poll (2000), two thirds of all people with disabilities are unemployed, and 81% of people with severe disabilities are unemployed. In examining employment by age, the Harris poll found that only 23% of people with disabilities between the ages of 45 and 64 years were working either full- (16%) or part-time (7%). Women with disabilities have the lowest rate of employment among all categories of disability and among all groups of individuals seeking work (Doren & Benz, 2001). In a U.S. national sample of all women with disabilities, Altman (1996) found that 45.2% of them were employed, and only 22.7% of women with severe disabilities were employed, as compared with 72.6% of women without disabilities. McNeil (1997) found that 24.7% of females with severe disabilities are employed. Szalda-Petree and associates (1999) found that women with disabilities are three times less likely to be employed than women or men in the general population.

Once employed, women with disabilities are the lowest paid of any group of workers (Crewe & Clarke, 1996). On average, the mean monthly income earned by employed women with disabilities was just more than

$1,200, as compared with men with disabilities whose monthly income was just more than $2,000 (Altman, 1996, p. 50). Women with disabilities earn 49% of the monthly earnings of men without a disability.

Given that employment income is not a viable source of financial security for people with disabilities, various forms of public or private funds must provide the safety net. According to the Harris Interactive poll (2000), 50% of adults with disabilities reported that they receive government financial benefits and insurance. Within that 50%, 18% of the respondents indicated that all of their income came from government benefits. In examining financial supports by degree of disability, 59% of individuals with moderate to severe disabilities reported that all of their income came from government benefits. When examining benefits by gender, the poll found that women have lower participation rates for the Supplemental Security Income program (25.6% versus 30.6%) and they receive lower premiums for Social Security Disability Insurance ($555 versus $672 per month) than their male counterparts. In a quality-of-life study of people with developmental disabilities in Ontario, Canada, Brown, Raphael, and Renwick (1997) discovered that 93.6% of their sample of 500 adults received financial support from family members and/or government programs. Altman (1996) also found that women with disabilities compose a large proportion of individuals covered by Medicaid, those receiving cash assistance, and those receiving housing assistance (44%, 50%, and 34%, respectively).

Economic Control

Few studies have directly examined the issue of control of finances for people with disabilities. Although the self-advocacy and self-determination movement is growing across the world for people with disabilities, it appears that the majority of individuals with intellectual disabilities do not control their own finances. Most individuals in the United States still have guardians for financial management, if not for all decision-making activities. In a Colorado study on quality of life, Sands and Kozleski (1994) found that only a few adults with disabilities did their own banking, paid their own bills, or made decisions about what to buy with their discretionary spending money (16%, 13%, and 35%, respectively). In the Canadian study on quality of life (Brown, Raphael, & Renwick, 1997), respondents were directly asked who controlled their finances. Of individuals who lived in congregate facilities, 95% in large facilities and 87% in small facilities said that someone other than themselves controlled all of their finances. Of individuals who lived with family members, 84% reported that their finances were not in their control. As would be expected, individuals who lived independently fared best. However, only 30%

of them indicated that they controlled all of their resources, while another 31% indicated that they jointly controlled their finances with someone else. In a study of older people with intellectual disabilities in Australia, Ashman, Hulme, and Suttie (1990) found that 80% of the respondents were totally dependent on others for handling money and that 77% of them were totally dependent for banking.

DISABILITY, SUPPORT SYSTEMS, AND PERSONAL SAFETY NET

People with disabilities depend on their formal and informal support networks to meet some of their most intimate and basic needs, including shelter, personal care, housekeeping, and community services. Too often, these support networks seem to function independently of the timelines and wishes of the person being supported. Structures are put into place to facilitate the family's or the residential program's needs. For example, the simple and personal decision about when to take a bath is too often dictated by a household schedule instead of the desires of the bather.

Safety nets are precarious in the lives of people with disabilities. The nets are only as strong as the success of their creators, who must weave together a support system from the complex interplay of personalities, policies, situational dynamics, and demography that exist in the human service arena. As people with disabilities age, they become even more dependent on their pieced-together safety nets, particularly as the safety nets evolve from informal networks to include formal, paid providers. Due to the escalating growth in the aging population in general and in the disability population specifically, this need for a more extensive formal support network is emerging at the very same time as the looming crisis in the direct care industry. Turnover in the industry is hovering between 60% and 75% per year, with many direct care workers leaving jobs in fewer than 30 days. Turnover in the service sector translates into impersonal and instable supports for people with disabilities. For aging people with disabilities, who often are just entering the formal support network in their later years, this crisis is a major challenge to their quality of life.

Living Arrangements

Worldwide, institutional living among individuals with disabilities has steadily declined. In most industrial countries, the majority of individuals with developmental disabilities live in the community, in a variety of situations. Specifically for the United States, 61% of people with disabilities live at home with their family; 29% live in their own homes; 6.1% live in group homes; and 0.7% live in large congregate facilities. The remaining 3.2% live in hospitals or institutions (Braddock, 2002). Ireland has slightly lower rates of family living than the United States, with 46.7% living in family homes (Mulvany & Mulcahy, 2002). In analyzing the demographic characteristics of people with intellectual and developmental disabilities who live in their own homes or with family members, Larson and her associates (2001) used data from the 1994–1995 U.S. National Health Interview Survey Disability Supplement (NHIS-D). They found that 18.1% of adults with disabilities lived alone or with an unrelated person, 9.3% lived with a spouse, and 72.6% lived with a relative (e.g., parent, sibling).

Residence by Age

In one study of living arrangements for people with intellectual disabilities, Seltzer (1985) found a range of percentages across studies, based on sample location and age range. As a general rule across all studies, she found that the percentage of people with disabilities who lived with their families was lower in older cohorts. These findings reflect global trends toward out-of-home placements as family caregivers and members with disabilities age. Ashman, Hulme, and Suttie (1990) examined living arrangements in Australia for a sample of adults with disabilities who were older than 50. They found that adults who lived in rural areas tended to live with family members (42.1%), in their own homes (10.5%), or in nursing homes (31.6%), while adults who lived in metropolitan areas tended to live in group homes (45.2%), large campus residences (29.0%), or family homes (6.5%). Bigby (2000a), in a study of older Australians with intellectual disabilities, found that nearly two thirds of the sample who were older than 65 lived in residential facilities for older people, such as elder congregate homes, nursing homes, and eldercare facilities. In a population study of older adults with disabilities in New Zealand, Hand (1994) found that 58% of them lived in a variety of community settings. However, individuals who were categorized with severe intellectual disabilities were much more likely to be living in public hospitals. Anderson, Gill, and Brown (2000) specifically examined living arrangements for women with intellectual disabilities and found that fewer than 20% of women older than 30 live in either a family home or their own home or apartment.

Support Systems

The majority of people with disabilities use some combination of formal and informal support systems. *Informal supports* are generally defined as unpaid supports that are provided by family members, friends, and neighbors. Various authors have defined *informal supports* in terms of their three traditional components: physical tending, material and psychological support, and general concern about the person's welfare (Bulmer, 1987; Dalley, 1988; Hooyman, 1983; Land, 1995; Seltzer & Krauss, 1994). In the disability field, as in the field of gerontology, mothers and other female relatives tend to provide the bulk of informal support. *Formal supports* are generally defined as paid supports that are provided by voluntary or government agencies and programs. In the disability field, such supports generally include residential care, respite, employment, life skills, day activity programs, transportation, guardianship, and advocacy.

The nature and extent of an individual's support network change as a variety of personal, situational, and demographic factors intersect (Bigby, 2000a; Krauss, Seltzer, & Goodman, 1992). For children and young adults with disabilities, the family is the primary source of physical, emotional, and material support. Unless extreme extenuating circumstances exist such as severe behavior problems, families tend to use the formal support system for very specific and limited services, such as respite care and advocacy. As the family ages and physical care becomes more burdensome, limited formal supports for some ADLs and transportation may be added to the network. However, families prefer that physical care and emotional support be provided through an extended informal network rather than through paid staff. In terms of day activities, older parents tend to keep their adult offspring with disabilities with them during the day, including them in the parents' activities rather than extending their friendship and activity sphere to a larger community (Seltzer & Krauss, 1994). Younger families who have young adults exiting the mandated education system often turn to formal supports for day programs, including employment and recreation. However, parents tend not to consider out-of-home living arrangements until they are facing their own physical decline or death (Heller & Factor, 1993). Often, extensive and more comprehensive formal support services are not brought into the person's support network until a crisis emerges.

Activities of Daily Living and Instrumental Activities of Daily Living

According to Anderson and colleagues (2000), approximately 41% of women with intellectual disabilities who are older than 30 years report that they are independent in personal care. With regard to other activities of daily living (e.g., eating, travel within the house), 83% of the women report they are independent. Instrumental activities of daily living (IADLs) (e.g., preparing meals, shopping, using the telephone, doing housework) proved to be more difficult for these women. Only 31% said they were independent in these areas. Ashman and his colleagues (1990) found similar results for Australians older than 50 who had mild and moderate intellectual disabilities. However, with regard to IADLs, more than 50% of this group of older people were totally dependent on caregiver help to do such activities as laundry, cooking, and using the telephone, as compared with 30% in the younger group. Brown and associates (1997) found that among Canadian adults with disabilities, approximately 50% needed help with ADLs, across all types of living arrangements.

Reliability and Crisis in Direct Care

A growing body of literature documents the fact that a crisis is emerging in direct care within the global population of people in need of long-term care (Fujiura & Yamaki, 2000; Turnham & Dawson, 2003). In the United States, government statistics indicate that by 2010, the need for paid support staff will increase by 45%. By specifically studying the issue of long-term care for adults with developmental disabilities in rural areas of the United States, Traci, Szalda-Petree, and Seninger (1999) found that there was a 66% turnover in personal assistants (i.e., direct care workers) over a 2-year period. They also found that individuals who had experienced turnover in personal assistance had significantly more secondary conditions that limited their participation in ADLs, increased their visits to hospital emergency rooms, and resulted in more days of hospitalization than people who did not experience such a turnover. In addition, people who experienced turnover had significantly more injury-related secondary conditions than individuals without a change in personal assistance. Turnham and Dawson (2003) found that the turnover in direct care workers resulted in inadequate and unsafe care, disconnected and impersonal care, the denial of basic care needs due to lack of staff, and increased risk due to being left without care.

FINDINGS FROM OUR STUDY

In order to gain more information about the economic and personal safety nets in the lives of the older women whom we interviewed, we asked them a variety of questions related to their finances, employment history, living arrangements, and formal and informal support networks. Findings in each of these dimensions of the safety nets are described in the following sections.

Sources of Financial Support and Personal Control of Resources

The majority of women across the 18 countries in our study indicated that they have a mixture of sources of financial support. More than half of the women indicated that they receive some type of government assistance, such as Supplemental Security Income in the United States, survivor pension in Taiwan, or government income supports in Canada. Other overlapping sources of financial support included wages (mostly from sheltered workshop activities), their husbands' employment, funds from their parents or siblings, family trust funds or parental pension funds, and retirement programs. When asked for their annual income, the majority of women did not know the answer to this question. Of the 40 who did know, only nine women had yearly incomes more than $10,000.

On average, between 40% and 50% of the women indicated that they manage their own money, but only about one quarter of the women in Taiwan and Japan indicated that they managed their own money. In examining the management of money by living arrangements, women who lived with their families and those who lived in congregate settings reported the least control of their money. Women who lived independently reported the most control of their money, and yet just over half of those women reported that they fully managed their own money. The management of money did not seem to be dependent on the age of the women. Across all age categories, approximately half of each age group indicated that they did not manage their own money. However, not surprisingly, the trend was for women to report less control with age, so that the oldest women tended to have the least control of their financial resources among the three age groups.

Employment

Nearly two thirds of the women we interviewed (66%) indicated that they had, at some point in their lives, worked for money. However, very few women still went to any type of work on a daily basis, and the work that they did was most often at a sheltered workshop or day activity program. With regard to age trends and employment, the majority of the oldest women in the study reported that they had worked for money during their lifetimes, as compared with two thirds of each of the other age groups. In examining who had worked by living arrangement, we discovered a clear trend toward increased employment by independence in living arrangement. Women who live in institutions tended to have the least employment history, followed by women who live in group homes, and women who lived in their own homes or family homes. It is most probable that living arrangement is serving as a proxy for level of disability, with women living in institutions having more challenging needs and therefore being least likely to be considered employable. Categorizing employment experience by regions of the world in which these women lived produced no discernable differences.

The women in the study reported that they worked an average of 26 hours per week, with a range of 2–48 hours. As is typical of women with minimal education in general and of women with disabilities in particular, these women tended to work in light assembly (42.3%) and service (57.7%) occupations. There were no differences in types of jobs by age cohort or geographic region. Women who lived independently were most likely to be working in service sector jobs. Though the numbers were small overall, women who lived in institutions tended to do assembly tasks.

The light assembly jobs were most often done in sheltered workshop settings. Examples of assembly tasks included sorting and assembling small parts, packaging parts for manufacturing, and cleaning industrial parts. Women in these occupations talked about the tedium and repetition of the work and the sometimes extremely low wages that they received. Women who worked in the service sector had a wide variety of jobs. The majority of these jobs involved commercial cleaning and housekeeping in such places as hotels, department stores, hospitals, schools, and voluntary organizations (e.g., Salvation Army). Jobs in the food industry were the next most frequently identified jobs, including both food preparation and dishwashing. These jobs were done in a variety of settings, including schools, volunteer organizations, and catering businesses. A small number of women talked about having been paid to do some knitting and sewing tasks, such as a Taiwanese woman who said she made doll clothes in a factory. A few women indicated that they had done farm work or small clerical tasks. One woman said she had worked as a child care assistant.

Although many women indicated that they had done a variety of jobs in their lives, no one had a career orientation or skill ladder structure to their employment. As one woman said, "I started different jobs after school at a furrier, sweet factory, laundry, then an occupational center. Didn't like that. [I] went to a day activity center and than a center for old people. Jobs only lasted a couple of weeks." These women appeared to be isolated in their employment. Overall, these women sat in anonymous rows of workbenches in noisy warehouses doing repetitive, menial tasks without any sense of the gestalt of their work. Hour after hour, they would sort small parts and put them in bags or clean tooled parts, not knowing how their work fit into a larger whole, such as a car or lawnmower motor. One woman, who is in her mid-sixties, described her job as follows:

> I use wet wipes to clean the grease off the big part, and then I put it in the bag, and then I clean the small part and put it in the bag. Some days my fingers crack to blood, and they get so cramped up I can't

unfold them. Look at my fingers—it's sad. [She moans and shakes her head.] I used to play the piano when I was a girl, but now look. [She shows her knuckles, which are bent in a seemingly permanent grasping position.] I have to keep using those wipes. Sometimes I just want to forget that grease.

Women who worked in service jobs were most often in positions hidden from the public—washing dishes, peeling potatoes, or mopping hotel rooms. These were the women whom a restaurant customer might glimpse working over a hot sink when the commercial kitchen door was left open a moment too long or women who might be seen through a partially opened door in a hotel corridor. They were employees who had very limited opportunities to interact with people other than their immediate supervisors. One woman described this kind of work:

> I used to work over the pot sink. Elbow-deep in steaming water, my hands red and raw. They told me that one day I had a seizure and fell into the sink. That was the end of my employment. Now, I do little bits in the [work]shop.

Although many of the women did not like the specific job tasks that they had to perform, more than 90% of the women who worked said that they liked being employed. They found value in having a reason to wake up every day to do these jobs. Often, it was just a contact, a smile, or a word or two from a co-worker or supervisor. When asked what was the best thing about working, the women had a variety of responses, not atypical of any other worker in the world. For some women, work was important because it provided a regular opportunity to interact with other people. Reasons such as "the people were very nice," "people were friendly," "meeting people," "interpersonal relationships," and "being able to talk to people" were frequently given when we asked them what they liked most about working. Other women intimated that being able to work lessened the sense of isolation in their lives. Statements such as "I see people every day," "I am among people," and "I met my boyfriend there" emphasize the role that work played in helping them to be connected with others. For some women, money was their best motivation: "I like getting my paycheck." "I like to earn money to buy clothes." "I can have my own money." For women who have very little discretionary money in their lives or very little access or control of their money, the pocket change they could make at their piece-rate jobs was important. Some women talked about having a sense of independence and freedom when they were employed: "I can make my own decisions." "I can get out of the group living situation when I work." Even if the women were not making much money, many of them reported that they felt useful and feeling useful, in and of itself, was what they liked about working. Interestingly, the women who worked with children and people whom they perceived to be in more need than themselves most often reflected on the value of work in making a contribution in their lives. These women made statements such as "I like helping with the kids in the spastics society"; "I love working with kids in the hospital"; "I'm doing important things"; and "I get a great feeling of satisfaction." Finally, some women said that they liked learning new things: "When I worked, I learned everything." "I learned every day when I was working."

When we asked the women about the worst aspects of their jobs, many women said they had no complaints. However, others cited a variety of concerns. The most frequently voiced complaint was that their jobs were strenuous and repetitive. Not surprising, these complaints were most common for the light assembly jobs. Many statements illustrated how difficult the manual labor was for these women: "I had to stand too long." "My hands got messed up." "Sometimes I had to tie stems together, which hurts my arms and hands and I felt like they were burning." "I had to carry crates of apples and oranges." "I have pain in my back from sitting on my knees and carrying heavy cartons." Other women reflected on the temperature-related stresses of their jobs. An Asian woman said she did not like filleting fish in the cold, while a British woman said that in hot weather soldering was the worst.

After complaints about the physical strain of their jobs, the women most often cited the emotional and psychological stresses they experienced. They talked about stress from co-worker interactions (e.g., "Sometimes they won't leave me alone"; "Pressure from everywhere made me nervous"; "The boys would bother me"), and then they talked about a lack of supervisor support. Three comments from three different continents illustrate the difficulties some of these women experienced with their supervisors. An American woman said, "I constantly tell them I need more help, but they tell me it's a one-person job," while an Argentine woman said, "I have to use numbers to count and I don't understand numbers," and a Scottish woman said, "I was left all alone with all the dishes to do on my own." One Belgian woman summed up the experience for many of these women by saying, "Once you have been working there for a while, it is not that nice, anymore." Finally, women from all corners of the world weighed in on the issue of low pay, with such complaints as "It was bad wages back then"; "I only got 50 cents a day"; and "I didn't get paid much."

Living Arrangements

Overall, women in the study lived in a variety of settings, with the single largest group of women (43.6%) living independently in apartments (25.5%) or in their own homes (18.1%). The second most common living arrangement was a group home (35.6%). Less than 20% of the women reported that they lived in a family home, whether with their parents, siblings, or extended family members such as aunts or uncles. Finally, less than 5% of the women reported that they lived in institutions.

Table 5 presents living arrangements by geographic regions. A few interesting trends emerged by regions of the world. Women in North America and Oceania most frequently lived in group homes, while women in Europe and Asia were more likely to live independently. Many of the Asian women lived in their own homes as they also were the largest single group of women to be married. No South American women lived in either group homes or institutions. All of these women either lived in family homes or independently. In the North America group also, no women were living in institutions.

When examining living arrangement by age, we noticed several trends. As presented in Table 6, with increased age, there is a trend toward more congregate living and less independent living arrangements. However, family living appears to remain stable across the age cohorts. The second trend was for the younger women in the study to still live with their families instead of living independently. No women in the youngest group lived in institutions, which appears to be consistent with the policies and philosophies of normalization and community integration that have been established since the 1980s.

The majority of women who lived in their own houses or apartments (62.8%) paid rent instead of owning their homes, with the exception of women in South America. More than 90% of those women owned their house or apartment. Ownership by age did not differ across the countries. When we asked women how long they had lived in their current living arrangement, the range of years was as diverse as the ages of the women in the study. The women reported that they had lived in their current residence anywhere from 1 year to 74 years, with an average length of stay of 14 years. The woman who had lived in the same place for 74 years was an American living in her family home. Concerning length of time in current residence by age, there was little variation from the mean for the group.

Table 5. Living arrangements, categorized by region

Region	Family home	Independent home	Group home	Institution
North America	10%	38%	52%	0%
Europe	14	50	33	3
South America	56	44	0	0
Asia	10	45	30	15
Oceania	6	29	59	6

Table 6. Living arrangements, categorized by age cohort ($N = 157$)

Age cohort	Family home	Independent home	Group home	Institution
40–55 years	18.2%	47.0%	34.8%	0 %
56–70 years	14.5	43.6	37.1	4.8
71+ years	17.7	23.5	41.2	17.6

When we examined time in residence by type of residence, we found quite a bit of variation. Women who live in their family homes had, on average, lived in one location the longest, at an average of 26 years, while women who lived in group homes had, on average, the shortest stay in one setting, at 7 years. Women who lived independently and in institutions had similar average lengths of stay, 15 years and 16 years, respectively. The fact that women who lived with their families had the longest stay in their setting is reflective of their lifelong arrangement. Conversely, the short period of time for group homes probably reflects two issues. First, as these women are aging and their caregivers are aging, they are moving into more congregate settings. Second, they are not living in one group home for extended periods of time. In fact, many women who live in such settings related that they are often being switched to new homes and care providers. Finally, concerning length of stay in current living arrangement by geographic regions, women in South America had the longest length of stay, at 26.3 years on average, while women in Oceania had the shortest length of stay, at 7.3 years on average. Again, the South America data reflect the fact that these women primarily lived in family homes. Women in North America, Europe, and Asia had similar lengths of stay, 12–14 years on average.

Approximately 20% of the women in the study lived alone. The majority of other women lived with one to four other people (58%). However, there was a wide range in the number of people who lived in the same residence (up to 37 people), with an average number of 3.5 co-residents. In descending order, these co-residents included housemates, spouses, extended family members, parents, caregivers, the women's children, and significant others. The women in Asian countries were more often married and therefore lived with their spouses, and all of the women in South America lived with their families. The number of co-residents did not vary by age cohorts or geographic regions. As would be expected, there was variation in the number of co-residents by type of living arrangement. Women who lived independently tended to live with only one other person, while women in family settings lived with three other people, those in group homes lived with six others, and those women in institutions lived with an average of ten other women.

The vast majority of women (88.4%) reported that they were happy with their current living arrangement but not always content with their lack of choice with regard to their housemates. Overall satisfaction did not seem to vary by age, with the exception that all of the oldest women reported that they were very happy with their living arrangement. As reported above, the majority of women in this age group lived in congregate settings. Although this living arrangement is not universally associated with resident satisfaction, the women in the oldest cohort reported that they were happy in these settings because of the level of care that was provided, security, and the access to companionship. As one woman said, "I can't do for myself now, and I am afraid of falling and dying in the bathtub." Another woman from this age group said, "When I lived in my home, I worried all the time about someone coming in. I could not sleep. I am calmer here." Finally, another woman talked about companionship, "I am not lonely here. If I want to go by myself, I go into my room. But it is nice to have someone to eat with and to talk to when I want." By contrast, women in the middle-age group (56–70 years) who lived in institutions, were the least happy with their living arrangement.

In examining living arrangement by regions of the world, we found that women in Oceania were most happy with their living arrangement, followed by women in Europe and North America. Women in South America and Asia were least happy with their living arrangement, although as a whole approximately three quarters of these women expressed satisfaction with their situation.

Support Networks

Almost all of the women named more than one person whom they considered to be their primary support. Their support networks ranged in size from one to seven people, with the average size of the individual networks being three people. Just over half of the women (54.9%) indicated that a paid staff person provided their primary support. The other women relied on unpaid supporters. Among the unpaid supporters, the women indicated that they most frequently relied on their siblings, followed by their parents or spouses, their children, and finally their friends. The majority of women who had family support also used formal paid support for many of their needs. As the women became older, their support network became more formal, with just over three quarters of the women in the oldest age group reporting that an agency staff member was their primary support provider. Concerning support networks by regions, women in North America were more dependent on formal, paid support providers, and women in South America were dependent solely on family caregivers. As would be expected, women who lived in family homes relied on family caregivers, and women who lived in group homes relied on agency staff. Interestingly, women who lived independently relied on a mix of formal and informal support providers. Those who continued to live independently even as they advanced in years shifted their care providers toward more formal networks.

The women, overall, had a wide range of needs for support. In terms of the amount of time they needed support, the number of hours ranged from less than 1 hour to 24 hours per day. The average amount of time they needed support was 8.9 hours per day. There were no substantial differences in the average amount of support time needed by age cohorts. When support needs were examined by living arrangement, an interesting pattern emerged. Women who lived independently needed the least amount of support at an average of 6.2 hours daily, followed by women who lived in institutions, at an average of 7.5 hours daily. Women who lived in group homes reported an average need of 11.1 hours of support, and women who lived in family homes reported an average need of 13.6 hours. Finally, concerning support need by geographic region, Asian women reported the highest need (13.8 hours), and European and Oceanic women were the most independent, at an average of 7 hours of support needed per day.

All of the women reported that their primary support person was reliable, and almost all of the women (93.5%) indicated that that support person was readily available to them. Nearly half (45.6%) reported that, in fact, that person lived with them. For others, their primary support person lived within 10 minutes of their residence. Reports on reliability, availability, and proximity did not vary by age, living arrangement, or region of the world. For a large number of the women, this sense of reliability and availability was fostered by access to various message systems. Comments like that from a woman in Ireland were indicative of this safety net support, "When I need something, I call my worker and leave a message. She usually calls me or comes around in less than 30 minutes."

Although the women reported that their support system was highly reliable, they did worry about high turnover within their networks. Women who lived in congregate care seemed to be particularly vulnerable to constant turnover in staff. As one woman said, "I don't even bother to learn their names anymore. Just as we get used to seeing them and they get used to our ways, they are gone." Another woman said, "Sometimes they [paid workers] yell at me and make me feel bad, but I just ignore it because I know they probably won't be back next week."

The women also worried about being left alone and the conditions that might precipitate or result from such isolation. In particular, they worried about their personal health, the health of their family members, their ability to continue to care for themselves, the possibility of being without support

when they needed it, the dangers of falling, and finally home entry and robbery. Across the three age groups, approximately 50% of each group of women
worried about being alone. Women who lived in family homes and in group
homes were least concerned about being left alone. Women who lived in
Europe and Asia were most afraid of being left alone. Although the majority
of women who lived in Asia reported that they lived with their spouses, they
also reported that their spouses were often away from home for rather long
periods of time, leaving the women to take care of the home and their farms.
Many of the Taiwanese women reported that their spouses would travel to
visit birth families in mainland China. Women who lived in their own homes
commonly made comments such as, "When everyone's gone and I haven't
done anything for a while, it's just that I feel all alone"; "Nobody's there"; "I
was in an apartment and when they don't come in, I worry. I need to be around
people"; and "I am worried I won't have someone come help me with my
papers, medical files, [and] accounts." Women who lived in family homes had
different types of worries: "Yes, I am worried about the future of my life. I'm
worried about if there is someone who can take care of me and my son."
"Sometimes I worry about when Mom and Dad may die, and I am afraid I
won't understand what is happening to me." One woman's comment about
her fears after the passing of one of her parents illustrates the concerns that
aging women with limited intellectual skills may face:

> Since my father died, I am afraid of the owls and that somebody will
> kill me. I am afraid of death. I saw my dead father, and I am afraid of
> it. I do not do anything if the staff is not there. They made me live
> upstairs, above them because I was afraid.

Finally, related to isolation and lack of support, many women expressed
the irrational belief that no matter what else happened in their lives, their
mothers would always be there for them. An older American woman who
lived in her own apartment said, "I worry that my sister will move, but I know
my mother will always be there," and a Norwegian woman said, "She [my
mother] always comes when I call."

Activities of Daily Living

The vast majority of women in this study were independent in ADLs. Most
women reported that they were self-sufficient in terms of their daily routines.
They had their own alarm clocks, awoke according to their schedules and
needs, bathed, dressed themselves, and began their days. Only a handful of
women said that they need assistance with selecting their clothes, washing

their hair, and dressing. Independence did not vary by living arrangement or geographic region.

Only when we asked the women to reflect on changes in their lives over the past 5 years did age-related changes in personal care begin to emerge. Eighteen women (11%) reported that they were less independent in IADLs than they were in the previous 5 years. The most common complaint was increased difficulty with mobility. Some women indicated that recent illnesses had limited their ability to care for themselves so that they needed more help from a primary care provider. Other women found that increased vision difficulties made the details of grooming tasks (e.g., attending to buttons, zippers, makeup, nails) more difficult, if not impossible. Finally, a few women indicated that recent bouts of depression had left them disinterested in their personal grooming. They did not lack the ability but rather the motivation.

Instrumental Activities of Daily Living

Table 7 presents the findings for independence in IADLs as reported by these women. The findings are presented for the entire sample and are then grouped by age, living arrangement, and regions of the world.

Overall, more than half of the women said they did their own shopping, cooking, housework, and laundry. Across the four activities, the women were least likely to report that they were independent in cooking. What is not possi-

Table 7. Instrumental activities of daily living, by percentage of independent activities

Groupings	Mean	Shopping	Cooking	Housework	Laundry
Sample	62.5%	66.2%	52.3%	65.6%	65.8%
Age cohort					
40–55 years	69.3	71	54	77	75
56–70 years	63.3	65	59	64	65
71+ years	35.5	53	22	28	39
Living arrangement					
Family	48.8	41	48	58	48
Independent	80.8	79	77	82	85
Group home	50.3	63	29	56	53
Institution	37.5	50	17	33	50
Region					
North America	58.5	60	50	61	63
Europe	64.8	72	60	65	62
South America	69.8	57	59	82	81
Asia	69.5	58	45	80	95
Oceania	44.3	69	28	41	39

ble to know from the interview is if these women did not cook because they had difficulty with the task or because they simply chose not to do so. If they are like the rest of the population, with the increased availability of prepared foods and active lifestyles, less of a premium is placed on traditional food preparation.

Not surprisingly, the women became less independent with age. However, it was not until the women passed the age of 70 that they were less independent than the average for the sample. By that age, the women in the oldest cohort were considerably less independent in all IADLs than their younger peers. As a cohort, all of the women in the youngest age group were above the group averages in all IADLs. With the exception of cooking, nearly three quarters of women in the youngest age group (40–55) reported that they did their own shopping, housework, and laundry. Just over half of these younger women reported that they did their own cooking. As the women moved into the next age group (56–70), just under two thirds of them were reporting independence in these activities. Just over half of the women in the oldest age group reported that they still were doing their own shopping, and less than 40% of them were doing their own laundry. Less than 30% were still doing housework or cooking.

In examining IADLs by living arrangement, we found that women who lived independently were also the most independent in their IADLs. Across all activities, they were well above the average for the entire sample of women. In all other living arrangements, the women were below the average across all activities. Not surprisingly, women who lived in institutions were least independent in cooking and housework. Women who lived in group homes and in family homes had interesting patterns of reported independence. Women who lived at home were less independent in shopping and laundry than women who lived in group homes or institutions, yet they were more independent in cooking and housework. These differences are probably more related to the nature of the environments and the expectations of the families and staff than to the ability or interests of the women.

Finally concerning difference by regions of the world, women in Oceania reported the least independence followed by women in North America. South American and Asian women were most independent, with European women following close behind. Although there were regional differences in independence levels for each specific IADL, it is not possible to know if this independence is more related to cultural expectations and preferences, residence requirements, or the actual skills and desired activities of the women themselves. For example, European women, who also were most likely to live independently, reported high levels of independence in shopping and cooking. Conversely, South American and Asian women, who were more likely to either live in family settings or be married, reported high levels of independence in housework and laundry.

For the women who were dependent on others for many of their IADLs, this dependence did not come without a price. Many of these women reported that in order to have their needs met, they had to sacrifice their freedom of choice regarding when and how activities would be accomplished. For example, some women reported that they had to wake up very early in the morning in order to take a bath according to the house schedule, which was set by the support staff, rather than taking a bath at their own leisure or desired time. When we asked what would be an ideal time for a bath, many women said before retiring for the night. When we asked if that was ever possible, one of the women said, "I was told I must take a bath at 4:45 A.M. When I don't take my bath, they write me up for misbehaving. I just don't want to get up on a cold morning and take a bath. I want to sleep." Another woman said that she has to go to the store when the van is leaving the group home: "Sometimes my feet ache or I don't have my check yet, but I have to go. No one can be left in the house. I don't want to watch other people shop. I know the next week what I need to buy will be on sale, but I have to buy it this week because that's when the van is going."

Just over half of the women indicated that walking is their most common mode of travel within their communities, followed by taking a public bus. About one third of the women said they most frequently travel by a private car (e.g., with a family member, friend, neighbor, staff person). Less than one quarter of the women use taxis, and only 3% of the women said they own a car. This travel mode hierarchy is probably reflective of the economic status of these women, in that they were more likely to use low or no-cost options instead of expensive taxis. Very few of the women reported that they were able to drive or had driven at any earlier age. Therefore, not only for economic reasons but also for practical ones, these women were not automobile owners. There were two interesting findings on travel by age. First, the youngest women tended to walk, the middle age group took the bus, and the oldest women relied on private cars. Very few younger women used private cars, and very few of the oldest women used the public bus system.

In examining community travel by living arrangement, we discovered several interesting patterns. The women who lived in family homes, as a group, used the public bus system most often. Across groups, these women were also most likely to be driven places in private cars. Women who lived independently were most likely to walk, and they were the most frequent walkers of all women across the various living arrangements. Frequency of use of the various modes of transportation by world regions indicated that Asian women were walkers, European women rode public buses, and Oceanic women took taxis or used private cars. Five women owned cars in the entire sample, four in Europe and one in Oceania. Rather than being related to their disability or other personal characteristics, their mode of travel was probably more a function of their culture and the availability of the various transportation options.

Desired Changes in Economic and Personal Safety Nets

The final question we asked women in this section of the interview was to speculate about what changes they wish that they could make in their safety nets. Six general themes emerged from their responses. Two themes were financially based, in that the women said they would like to have more expendable money for such uses as home repairs, dinner in a restaurant, clothing, or a vacation. Statements from several of the women highlighted the importance of small choices and the impact that those choices would make on the quality of their lives: "I would buy my own food." "I would buy what I want." "I would buy better bread." "I would buy clothes, bingo, and holidays." "I would get my hair done." "I would buy my own chocolate instead of my sister bringing it to me." "I would like to get a nice black shirt with sequins and a red top with sequins for my birthday party."

Three other themes addressed their personal concerns. For example, many women expressed the desire to move to a more independent living situation: "I wish I could live in an apartment with my boyfriend." "I'd have a different roommate." "I would like to live in a place of my own sometime before I die." "I would like to move." "I would like some help with changing my housemate." Some wished to get out and about more: "Sometimes I just want to go out and not have to cancel my activities and appointments." Others wanted to have access to more personal help. Several statements illustrated this desire for more support: "I wish I had more flexibility in when I receive support services—not just during the day but at night if I need it." "I would like to have someone come every day." "I would like to have my evening meal brought to me and not have to go out to get it." A final, overarching theme that was expressed by the women was that they wished they could be happier and less worried about everything. Underlying this expressed feeling of mild depression and anxiety was, again, a sense of their not being in control of their own lives. Too many of their basic needs and activities were dictated by their economic situation and their support providers.

SUMMARY

Consistent with the extant literature on women with intellectual disabilities, the women in this study were dependent on their external economic and personal safety nets for their existence. Like so many people with disabilities

worldwide, they are poor and dependent on a combination of government subsidies and family resources for their financial needs. Approximately half of the
women in this study reported that they make decisions about their resources;
however, it was not clear how aware they may be about the totality of the
resources that are in essence controllable. In reality, it appeared that the majority of these women were referring to the money they actually see and touch
on a daily basis. This pocket-money reality is more consistent with findings
from other international and longitudinal studies on control of resources
among people with disabilities. Regardless of the level of spoken control, all
of the women wished they had more actual money and more control of it.
They did not wish for big changes that more money could bring but little
extras that they perceived would change the quality of their lives. Although
more women indicated that they had worked during some period of their lives
than the typical population of women with disabilities, none of these women
talked about careers or longitudinal employment. Assembly and service jobs
were typical, and they were jobs that contributed little money, few opportunities for social interaction, or little status. These women did work that other
people did not want to do, and yet they all talked about how they liked to
work. Their work made them feel that they were important, contributing, and
learning participants in the world. For many of them, work was an opportunity to be a legitimate member of the society.

In terms of their personal safety nets, fewer lived in family homes than
other research studies have shown. In addition, the percentage of women living in family homes did not change with increasing age, which also was
inconsistent with the literature. However, age did increase congregate living
for these women, as the literature indicates. In this sample, the older women
tended to move from more independent arrangements to group or institutional living. The oldest women in the sample were not dissatisfied with such
living arrangements. They seemed to recognize their need to have more assistance, and they were afraid to be alone and lonely. Independent of what type
of living arrangement these women had, they all experienced high satisfaction
with their residence across ages, settings, and geographic regions.

As a group, these women appeared to be more independent in IADLs
than women with intellectual disabilities who are cited in previous studies.
Their independence did not appear to change significantly until these women
became quite old, consistent with normative aging in the general population.
Any marked differences in independence appeared to be more a function of
opportunity and expectations than true functioning ability or desire on the
part of the women to be more independent. Taking into account that 30 of
these women had raised 70 children and that many were married and had

maintained households, it is not surprising that they continued to be independent in life's daily activities. Independent or not in ADLs, all of these women acknowledged that they relied on formal and informal support networks to help them on a daily basis. With increased age, the networks tended to become more formal, with the majority of the women in the study reporting that they relied more on paid caregivers than their family, friends, or volunteers. In fact, family ties were an interesting construct for these women. Family was important for emotional support, but physical support was more likely to be provided by the service system.

CHAPTER FIVE

Health

A string of jewels
from a broken necklace,
scattering—
more difficult to keep hold of
even than these is one's life.

IZUMI SHIKIBU

Hazel is 60 and has lived in Australia all of her life. She is single and lives alone, currently renting her apartment from a government agency after years of living in an institution. These days, she relies on her best friend, Martha, and her case-worker, Sally, for support. She receives a disability pension, but she does not know exactly how much it amounts to. In addition she has a part-time job, and she speaks enthusiastically about her work: "I work as a peer educator with a women's health service—just when they need me." She likes her job very much. She gets to be with other people, earn money, and travel around the state where she lives. But she has been troubled lately because the position she holds needs agency funding, and she says, "It looks like there isn't any more."

Looking back, Hazel says that her childhood was hard: "We didn't have any money, and mum was sick. I don't really remember much—then I went with the sisters." At the residential school run by a religious order of nuns, Hazel received some years of formal education. She remembers these difficult times for her family vividly: "Well, we got taken away from my mum. She couldn't look after us. I had four sisters and a brother. Only my brother and I are still alive. I met him in the institution, and I didn't even know he was my brother."

In the past 5 years, Hazel has experienced two major changes: "I moved house. I was engaged and am not anymore." Asked what she would change about her current living or income arrangements, she replied: "To be able to cook using the stove. Since I had some trouble when I moved in with the stove, I have just been eating microwave dinners because they won't let me use the stove until I have learned how to. Sally is going to teach me to do this."

These days, Hazel has a quiet routine if she is not at work. "I get up and have some breakfast, some days I have meetings I have to go to in the city so I would catch a train in, like today. I watch TV if I don't have to go anywhere or do anything. I clean a bit and get some dinner and go to bed late."

Hazel says that she takes little medication, "A tablet for my moods, that's all." She does not do any physical exercise but admits that "I am on a diet now so I can't eat all the things I like." Watching television is Hazel's favorite activity, and she would change little about how she spends her leisure time: "Nothing, maybe go dancing." She takes a regular vacation, however: "Yes, about once a year, a group usually, go to the beach. Go places like Tasmania. The beach was really nice—a bit cold but fun. We went out for dinner. I have been to Tasmania. That was really nice. Good to see different places."

Hazel does not worry about being on her own. "No, I have got services, and I have got my good friend, Martha, who is always in touch with me and looks after me. I met her in the institution—she worked there and she is still my friend." Her friendships have not changed: "Not much only since leaving the institution you don't see them as much." And her support person "is with the council so if she can't come, someone else will." In addition, Hazel has regular contact with her brother: "I see Joe almost every day. I have got a nephew, but I don't see him." Her family circumstances have changed in the past few years: "Yes, Joe isn't very well now. He lives in a hostel, [and] they look after him." At the same time, Joe is the source of some of Hazel's few worries: "Really, sometimes I worry about Joe. I wish he wouldn't come and visit and eat all my food and drink my drinks."

What are the three most important things in Hazel's life today? "Working as an advocate and peer facilitator, living in my own place, seeing my friends." As a facilitator, she talks to people about their problems. Moving to her current home was the best thing in her life in the past few years, and the worst is the threat to her work. The secret to life, Hazel thinks, is that "it was great to get out of the institution and it's good to work in advocacy." She observed that girls with disabilities today "don't live in institutions. They live with their families and have a lot of friends." As for the future, she says, "[I] haven't really got any dreams. I used to want to get married but I don't now. I am too old." And looking ahead 5 years, Hazel concludes, "I will be 65 and still be much the same."

This chapter focuses on what health means in the lives of the participants in this study, 167 older women with intellectual disabilities living in 18 countries. Why did we place health at the center of our exploration of successful aging? Our aim was neither to document illness nor to cast women's lives in a medical mold. Rather, we wished to capture their positive experiences of growth and change from youth through middle and older adulthood. We also wished to hear an account of their history, environments, and patterns of living so as to understand more fully what factors may be associated with good or poor health outcomes. The 1,000-year-old Japanese poem at the beginning of this chapter captures the spirit of lifelong striving to keep hold of the precious but sometimes elusive elements of one's life and craft these into a whole.

Health lies at the heart of each person's satisfaction with life. It is the homespun flag unfurled to signal how the day goes and how one feels about being alive. In most cultures, asking about someone's health is a part of greeting that person. Conceptually, health and quality of life are close kin, rather than neighbors. The two constructs overlap: A good life enhances health and health indicates a good quality of life (Schalock & Verdugo, 2002). Not surprisingly, good health emerges at global, regional, and national levels as a legitimate goal for all citizens and thus a priority for policies.

Globally, it may be said that the world is living dangerously, with 10 risk factors accounting for an enormous amount of illness and death (World Health Organization, 2002). These factors include underweight, unsafe sex, high blood pressure, unsafe sanitation and hygiene, iron deficiency, obesity, and others. It seems that the key to change is to make sound information available, and individuals will make healthier, less risky choices. But not everyone has access to information in a form they can understand. Some ways to diminish health risks are beyond anyone's personal control (e.g., using clean water, addressing the environmental factors leading to obesity). In addition, poverty prevents many from taking steps to understand health risks and act accordingly. To be poor or disadvantaged is to face a greater burden of health risk (World Health Organization, 2002). Health is important because it is becoming increasingly possible to do something about improving it. At the system or country level, the World Health Organization's report recommended that priority should be given to controlling well-known, widespread risks for which "effective and acceptable" reduction strategies are available (2002, p. xvii).

Private experiences intersect with the public health domain. Although some aspects of health are accessible to public scrutiny or interventions, health is nonetheless experienced profoundly and personally throughout the lifespan. Personal health has a history, too. Many women interviewed in this study lived in institutions or in relative disadvantage as girls or young women. They missed opportunities as young adults to develop a healthy lifestyle through proper diet and exercise. Culture played its part. Growing to adulthood in seclusion during the 1950s in a country where good dentistry was not widespread literally left its mark on many older women with intellectual disabilities who were already vulnerable because of poor hygiene, diet, or long-term medication. In this way, people with intellectual disabilities are often invisible to formal health systems devised for the general population (Prasher & Janicki, 2002).

What do individuals report about the meaning of health in their lives? How does health status imprint everyday experience? How can we foster health promotion and prevention? What are the hallmarks of mastery in pursuing a healthy life? Such questions helped to shape this chapter of the story of resilience among older women with intellectual disabilities. This chapter presents what we learned from the women about their health in the light of published evidence. First, we review recent literature about core topics: gender, age, and other determinants of health; the health of women with intellectual disabilities; self-appraisals of health; and an overarching public health framework. Second, we define the quantitative and qualitative measures applied in this study during interviews with women themselves. Third, the findings related to women's health are presented, applying a multilevel model of health indicators borrowed from the public health domain. Finally, we discuss the results in a global context, where prosperity can pay the price of longer, healthier lives.

REVIEW OF LITERATURE

From a global view, life expectancy expresses health outcomes most starkly. Among the countries in our study, for example, citizens in Japan live an average of 81 years, in Australia 79.9 years, and in Canada 78.8 years (United Nations Development Programme, 2002). By contrast, those in Sierra Leone or Mozambique do not, on average, live to age 40. With few exceptions—Ireland being one (Mulvany & Barron, 2003)—basic demographic data about people with intellectual disabilities are not available in a form that permits comparisons by age and gender with the general population. Nor do health systems report data on their health status and outcomes comparably. One exception is the Netherlands, where people with intellectual disabilities may be identified on registers of primary care physicians (van Schrojenstein Lantman-de Valk, Metsemakers, Haveman, & Crebolder, 2002). In that country, comparable data on morbidity and mortality, at least, are available.

To present the relevant literature on health, gender, and aging among people with intellectual disabilities in this section, we first examine evidence for adopting a transactional model of health and focus on gender as a health determinant. Next, we present evidence on the health of people with intellectual disabilities, drawing on international reports and specifically on the health of women in this group and how aging influences health. We review key elements within a public health framework. And finally, we outline major categories of health indicators, shaping the way we report the findings on the elements of this study related to women's health.

Gender and Health

In each country and for all people, gender helps to determine health. The demographic forecast offers a striking example of the widening presence of women among older people in the near future: "By 2025 there will be more than 800 million older people in the world, two thirds of them in developing countries, and a majority of them will be women" (World Health Organization, 1998, p. 101). Health outcomes across cultures tell a complex story, albeit one with a familiar beginning: In most countries, women live longer than men. A larger group of older women live on to experience more years of life with lowered quality, often alone, because of their longer survival after the development of a disability or handicap (Robine et al., 1999). As women live longer than men, the quality of their longer life becomes a matter of central importance. Thus, promoting women's health includes an analysis of how different social roles, decision-making power, and access to resources affect health status and access to health care. The right of all women to the best attainable standard of health—as well as their right of access to adequate health services—is a primary consideration worldwide.

Notably, women outlive men in most parts of the world. In Italy, life expectancy is 81.6 years for women and 75.2 years for men. Women in Argentina expect to live an average of 77.2 years, outliving men by 7 years. In Norway, ranked highest worldwide in the *Human Development Index* (United Nations, 2002; see also Table 2), women outlive men by 6 years. In the United States, the gap between male and female life expectancy at age 65 has narrowed; women who reach 65 may expect to live another 19 years, while men may expect 16 further years (Merck Institute of Aging and Health & Gerontological Society of America, 2002).

But men and women differ also in the specific health conditions they are likely to experience, due in part to onset of sex-specific illnesses such as breast cancer among women and prostate cancer among men (Kerr, 2002; World Health Organization, 2002). In addition to distinctive patterns of health status and functioning, gender differences are also apparent across a range of health risk behaviors. Men and women show marked differences in health behaviors. Some are the result of the ways men and women grow and take on certain social roles and expectations for how to behave in their cultures. Addis and Mahalik (2003) reviewed the evidence on how men seek or do not seek help for a range of problems in living. They argued that men's help-seeking is best understood as a function of the way they are brought up and construe masculinity and how they perceive aspects of giving and receiving help. For example, men may be more likely to seek help if they believe they can reciprocate.

Moving Targets

Being healthy is a complex, dynamic state. This was a second core theme emerging from the varied array of publications we surveyed. Current approaches focus on the interplay of gender, age, and environment, as well as individual behaviors, in determining health. Newer concepts, such as *health gain,* set even more ambitious targets. Living in good health means more than the absence of disease: It means that men and women are supported to adjust to their environments, to prosper, and to make a contribution to the lives of others.

To do so means retaining one's functional capacities through adulthood. But evidence suggests that women spend more of their ultimately longer lives with limitations in everyday functioning. Pope, Sowers, Welch, and Albrecht neatly summarized how age, poverty, stress, and physical characteristics take their toll on women's health. These authors found that 20% of a very large sample of 16,065 women ages 40–55 years had functional limitations:

> Consistent with findings in older women, this study shows that in addition to health conditions, potentially modifiable risk factors including high body mass index, difficulty paying for basics, and high levels of stress are associated with physical functioning limitations of women at midlife. (2001, p. 494)

They concluded that behavioral and environmental risk factors associated with disease processes may be causal factors of systemic imbalances that can lead to adverse disease conditions for women.

Cobbs and Ralapati endorsed the importance of functional status in assessing older people's health, noting that older women are more likely than men to have chronic illnesses and disabilities:

> Measurement of health status becomes difficult in the presence of multiple chronic conditions. For this reason, studies of health in older persons often require assessment of functional status to detect need

for health services, measure change over time, and determine the effects on outcomes related to quality of life. (1998, p. 128)

Aging

Gender continues to determine health as people age. Less favorable status was especially notable among women surveyed in a large study conducted in the United States, with more than half of all elderly people reporting some difficulty in completing one or more functional tasks (Porrell & Miltiades, 2002). Regional differences emerged, and Porrell and Miltiades concluded that the harmful effects among older women living in one region—the states of the Deep South—were largely due to the region's lower population density and higher level of poverty. Their findings are consistent with those of Bierman and Clancy (2001), who analyzed data from the 1999 Medicare Health Outcomes Survey in the United States and found that older women who are least able to negotiate the health care system have the highest burden of illness. Women who were poor, who had less education, and who held minority group status were more likely to suffer from chronic diseases and limitations in functioning.

Mental health looms as a distinctive risk for older people. Heart diseases and signs of physical deterioration have a significant, negative effect on mental health, as does conjugal bereavement, a life event of great consequence for older people (Lindeboom, Portrait, & van den Berg, 2001). Porrell and Miltiades (2002), commenting that more than half of all older people report some difficulty in completing one or more functional tasks, found regional differences in functional status among aging people in the general population.

In summary, although women outlive men, they are more likely to live with disabilities or lowered functioning. The impact of gender on health is widespread, helping researchers to determine patterns of risk, status, and health behaviors, as well as outcomes. Poverty and socioeconomic status are also key determinants of health status.

People with Intellectual Disabilities

Knowledge of the health determinants of people with intellectual disabilities hovered at a modest level for much of the 20th century. This dearth of knowledge was associated with the removal of many people in this group to remote institutions, where they led invisible and relatively short lives. Since 1999, publication of important critical reviews of literature and health-related research has increased this knowledge. In the United States, the Surgeon General consulted a team of experts to identify strategies to reduce apparent health disparities for citizens with intellectual disabilities (U.S. Department of Health and Human Services, 2002). Elsewhere, Horowitz and colleagues (2000) prepared a critical review of health-related literature on this population. A set of reports on the healthy aging of adults with intellectual disabilities was prepared for the World Health Organization by the International Association for the Scientific Study of Intellectual Disabilities (IASSID) (2000). Subsequently, a series of books presented evidence on health issues for women with intellectual disabilities (Walsh & Heller, 2002), on the physical health of adults with intellectual disabilities (Prasher & Janicki, 2002), and on behavioral and mental health issues for this population (Davidson, Prasher, & Janicki, 2003).

Key risk factors for ill health among people with intellectual disabilities have been documented, such as inadequate nutrition, need for medication, and lack of exercise (Beange, 2002). For example, Messent and Cooke (1998) reported low levels of cardiorespiratory fitness and physical activity and high levels of overweight in a sample of adults in the United Kingdom. Health system factors also have a bearing on the health of people with intellectual disabilities. Often, primary care health professionals do not have training to ensure that they will communicate effectively with these individuals or their family members. Health professionals receive little training to facilitate their contacts with older women with intellectual disabilities (Gill & Brown, 2000). And family members may lack information about how to promote their relative's health. Clinicians may find that continuity of care across sectors (e.g., primary care and mental health care) is fragmented. Crucially, men and women with intellectual disabilities themselves lack the skills needed to pursue healthy lives.

For people with intellectual disabilities, compromises to their health arise at different levels. They may have conditions amenable to treatment but nonetheless untreated or untreated specific health issues related to the individual disability. In addition, they may fail to gain from generic health promotion, such as blood pressure screening (Kerr, 2002). Mental health problems may be masked by the presence of developmental or other disabilities and hence elude treatment (Thorpe et al., 2001). Antecedent conditions may include life stressors, limited social networks, and fewer opportunities for social learning. Also, adverse reactions may be exacerbated among adults with intellectual disabilities due to cognitive impairments, poor self-esteem, and relatively poor social support.

Longer life brings health risks as well as opportunities. For example, longevity for people with intellectual disabilities is matched by an increased risk of cardiovascular disease (Turner & Moss, 1996), one of the main causes of death among people in this population. Greater life expectancy also gives rise to interactions of older age-onset conditions with those acquired in child-hood or young adulthood. In addition, specific populations have particular health risks as they age: higher rates of cardiovascular disease and diabetes arising from morbid obesity among those with Prader-Willi syndrome, for example. Knowledge of the specific age-related health risk factors associated with this and other syndromes is essential in enhanced prevention or early diagnosis. Some groups have specific vulnerabilities: Older adults with Down syndrome are more likely to develop Alzheimer's disease (Janicki & Ansello, 2000). Yet, Burt and colleagues (1995) concluded that apart from occurrence of a progressive dementia such as Alzheimer's disease, the adults with Down syndrome in their study displayed minimal age-related functional change. Older people may not have ready access to regular screening for sight and hear-ing deficits. And many adults may have unidentified—and thus untreated—mental health conditions.

As they age, adults with intellectual disabilities experience health risks that are more like those of their peers. In a Finnish study, individuals with a mild level of intellectual disability had similar mortality patterns to the gen-eral population (Patja, Molsa, Iivanainen, & Vesala, 2001). Patja and col-leagues commented that as people with intellectual disability move from institutions to the community, they are exposed to similar environmental risks to the general population, including shortage of health care resources. This heightened exposure—rather than community settings themselves as an inde-pendent risk factor—and lack of prevention compel health professionals to promote health in the community and decrease avoidable mortality by pre-venting accidents, infections, and cardiac diseases (Patja et al., 2001).

Finally, the cultural identities of people with intellectual disabilities are often overlooked in the haste to apply an administrative or diagnostic label. But each person has a birthright to be a member of his or her own culture, a right expressed with some force in the United Nations' *Standard Rules* (1994). In this study, we discerned surface features differing across cultures, for exam-ple, in the words spoken or the foods the women liked to eat. But we inferred that cultural waters ran very deeply: that real differences in what is expected of women and of people with disabilities underlie the women's accounts of their life experiences. It may be assumed that these cultural filters helped to determine the women's experiences of health.

Women's Health

Gender helps to determine health for people with intellectual disabilities, as for other individuals. Life expectancy has increased for this population: Those with mild or moderate levels of intellectual disability are likely to live longer and are thus more likely to incur age-related conditions similar to those in the general population (Janicki, Dalton, Henderson, & Davidson, 1999). Men and women with intellectual disabilities thus experience health risks associated not only with their gender but also with conditions related to the presence of intellectual disability. Women with intellectual disabilities, for example, have particular life experiences and risks to their reproductive and sexual health (van Schrojenstein Lantman-de Valk, Metsemakers, et al., 2002). Individuals in this group have poor literacy skills, and consequently they do not often have access to information on menstrual hygiene, sexually transmitted diseases, contraception, and related topics. Nor do these women have equal access to screening programs for breast or cervical cancer. Men with intellectual disabilities, too, have specific health risks. These include increased rates of morbidity and mortality—due to biological factors, harmful health behaviors, and poor access to health care (Kerr, 2002).

Disparities in health are evident when people with intellectual disabilities are compared with their peers in the general population (U.S. Department of Health and Human Services, 2002). In a Dutch study, for example, men with intellectual disabilities appeared to contract sexually transmitted diseases eight times more often than their peers without disabilities (van Schrojenstein Lantman-de Valk, Metsemakers, et al., 2002). Robertson and colleagues (2000) found that most of the men (84%) and women (88%) in a study of 500 adults with intellectual disabilities living in residential settings in the United Kingdom were physically inactive—levels equivalent to those reported for people 75 years and older in the general population. Furthermore, physical inactivity was associated with residents' lower ability and more restrictive residential settings. Women residents were more likely to be obese.

A complex array of factors may heighten a woman's risk for a particular condition. For example, the risk of osteoporosis is greater among older women with intellectual disabilities, who may experience a regimen of anticonvulsant medication, poor nutrition, a sedentary lifestyle, and earlier menopause. And women with Down syndrome experience an earlier menopause than women who have intellectual disabilities but who do not have Down syndrome and those in the general population (Schupf et al., 1997). In addition, women with intellectual disabilities may not receive information on sexual and reproductive health matters—such as menopause—in a form that they understand (van Schrojenstein Lantman-de Valk, Schupf, et al., 2002).

Women with intellectual disabilities incur other risks to their health and safety. They have a higher risk for various forms of abuse. Research suggests that interventions should take into account the cultural environment and living and working conditions as well as the individual's characteristics (Walsh & Murphy, 2002). Preventing abuse and offering appropriate treatment to women who have been abused are also important in promoting mental health among women with intellectual disabilities (Lunsky & Havercamp, 2002). These authors conclude that our current understanding of the prevalence of mental health conditions and of strategies to heighten mental health for women is incomplete.

For their part, older women with intellectual disabilities may find it difficult to grasp the meaning of life course changes without validation from others. In a series of focus groups carried out with women in several countries, it emerged that many struggled to understand their own experiences of aging and what this process means (Walsh, Heller, Schupf, & van Schrojenstein Lantman-de Valk, 2001). It may be that the women were buffered by seclusion or service systems from being members of their own communities. As a result, many lost opportunities to pass through life stages typical for their peers—leaving school, taking up productive work, marrying, becoming a parent, managing a household, and identifying themselves as middle-age or older adults with distinctive roles. A woman who has a patchy understanding of her status in her own society and her stage of the lifespan may not be expected to identify appropriate health risks and promotion strategies.

In summary, disparities are evident in risk and vulnerability, health status, and access to health screenings and care available to women with intellectual disabilities. At the level of health systems, women in this group may simply be invisible to generic initiatives in their countries. A public health framework is applied to aspects of the health of women with intellectual disabilities in the next section.

PUBLIC HEALTH

The visibility of people with intellectual disabilities on the public health screen varies from nation to nation. Even within the European Union of member states, a prosperous region with shared social policy objectives, diverse forms of support for people with intellectual disabilities have developed to reflect national policies and traditions. Nations have adopted varied approaches in monitoring the health of people with intellectual disabilities (Walsh, Kerr, & van Schrojenstein Lantman-de Valk, 2003). In some countries, the approach is embedded in the mainstream of their country's health service system: one system serves all. But elsewhere, people with intellectual disabilities form a special subgroup and information about their health—or other life experiences—may never reach public scrutiny. Disparities in health may not be recorded at all, and thus there is no basis for tracking any changes over time. Without agreed indicators, it is not possible to make international comparisons in reducing disparities for people with intellectual disabilities, nor for other population subgroups (Starfield & Shi, 2002).

Inequalities in health status are a core target for public health interventions:

> The more recent emphasis in public health on inequalities and the influence of social determinants on health outcomes highlights awkward questions about who has benefited most from public health and health promotion activities, as evidence has emerged of interventions that have widened health inequalities as a result of health promotion campaigns. (Waters & Doyle, 2003, p. 72)

We do not have enough evidence to chart the impact of, or benefits from, public health campaigns on women with intellectual disabilities, nor to compare these women with their peers in the general population in terms of the effects of public health campaigns. This is itself a fruitful area for research, especially as exploring the interplay of the public health domain with personal experiences can potentially illuminate what is important in promoting good health. As Oakes and Rossi suggested,

> [P]ublic health research aims to investigate how levels of inequality and variation in social context affect health outcomes. SES [socioeconomic status] measures for public health may thus need to capture more of the social context than the indexes of income, education or occupational position can offer. Indeed, it is the richness of the embedded social context (i.e., networks and environment) that public health researchers appear most interested in. (2003, p. 773)

These authors proposed a more complex conceptualization of socioeconomic status to capture material, human, and social forms of capital in order to explain how individuals realize health goals. But to chart such a process over time demands useful, reliable measures of diverse factors related to health.

Health indicators are the attributes that may be measured to express the health of a population and make it possible to record change over time and to make comparisons across populations. A recent model was devised to promote more cohesive health monitoring and comparisons within the 15 European Union countries, identifying a set of health indicators under four categories that apply to the general population (ECHI Project Working Group, 2001):

1. Demographic characteristics

2. Health status

3. Health determinants

4. Health systems

In 2002, a new project, Pomona, began work to see if these indicators might usefully apply to individuals with intellectual disabilities (Walsh et al., 2003).

The first category, demographic characteristics, describes familiar measures that are taken for granted in national census data but are often not recorded for people with intellectual disabilities. Health status indicators comprise the second category. Both men and women with intellectual disabilities have particular vulnerabilities to disorders and illness. They may experience co-morbidity of conditions (e.g., hypothyroidism, obesity, and epilepsy) or psychiatric illnesses that persist without being diagnosed or treated. In the United States, reports of health status made by older people in the general population vary by age as well as by race. Overall trends in self-reports are positive: The percentage of those ages 65–74 who reported excellent or very good health rose from 35% in 1982 to 42% in 1999 (Merck Insitute of Aging and Health & Gerontological Society of America, 2002). By contrast, older men and women with intellectual disabilities may not be encouraged to form self-appraisals, either of their own health or their standing in society. Yet, subjective social status (i.e., a person's belief about his or her location in a status order) is a strong predictor of ill health, a finding that expresses the multidimensional nature of both social inequality and health (Singh-Manoux, Adler, & Marmot, 2002). We do not have the evidence to be confident about how older people with intellectual disabilities rate their health or social status when compared with their peers without disabilities.

Health determinants emerge at different levels: individual, behavioral, socio-economic, environmental, or cultural contexts. The impact of obesity, iron deficiency, and the other global risk factors identified by the World Health Organization (2002) have to date been less systematically applied to the health of people in this group. They may, in addition, have few opportunities to promote healthy patterns of nutrition and physical exercise (Heller & Marks, 2002; Robertson et al., 2000). Achieving a balance between self-determination and the exercise of choice presents a challenge to those who wish to promote the health of older people with intellectual disabilities (Turner & Hatton, 1998).

Health systems vary a good deal in whether and how they chart the health of citizens with intellectual disabilities. Observers may speculate that policy makers leave well enough alone for fiscal reasons. In their discussion of best practice in health care and European health care systems, Perleth, Jakubowski, and Busse (2001) suggested that such guidelines may increase costs because they recommend effective treatment for conditions previously untreated—especially so for older people with disabilities.

The overarching public health framework includes an array of health indicators at individual, socioeconomic, health system, political, and environmental levels. Reflecting complexity and given the cross-cultural sweep of this study, we chose sets of quantitative and qualitative measures to explore the health experiences and beliefs of the women we interviewed. These are described in the next section.

MEASURES OF HEALTH

Many factors contribute to health. Accordingly, we chose a range of measures at different levels to capture aspects of the health of the women who took part in this study. Adopting a contextual model of health, we asked the women to describe their current health status—how they felt, how they rated their own health, and whether any condition kept them from doing what they wished. We asked, too, about diet, exercise, and some other behaviors that help to determine health. To explore their standing in their community's health service system, we asked about their recent contact with health care professionals.

Quantitative measures reflected the four categories of health indicators discussed in the previous section. Demographic data included information about the women's age, social status, educational background, living conditions, and primary form of support (e.g., from family member or professional support worker). Health status indicators ranged from self-rankings of health to the presence of problems in hearing, vision, mobility, and other functional capacities and specific medical conditions or diseases. The determinants of health were indicated at the level of health behavior (e.g., diet and exercise) and by access to preventive health screenings. Finally, we sought information about the women's contact with health care service systems. To explore the women's personal experiences of their own health, we invited them to tell us in more detail about a number of health-related topics, such as medications, favorite activities, and patterns of regular exercise.

From the first, we knew that the women spoke to us with distinctive voices and that their lifelong experiences would reflect the expectations of women of their age and situation held by people in their own cultures. We knew that these cultural and historical filters would influence the women's understanding of their health in middle and older adulthood. We heeded the example set by Ingstad and Whyte, in their book *Disability and Culture,* who said that they wished to be "wary of a pitfall of cultural juxtaposition: our tendency to look at other cultures in terms of our own problems and thus to fail to grasp the premises upon which other people are operating" (1995, p. 5). This sound advice helped us to remain sensitive to the assumptions the women in our study made in giving an account of their health. Nordic women spoke with regret about country hikes and skiing, pastimes now perhaps beyond reach. Women in Asian countries mentioned regimens such as tai chi and herbal remedies as preferred options for keeping healthy. North American women were deft at naming brand-name medications. Yet in all parts of the globe, women seemed not to fix on one element or intervention as being responsible for their health to date. Rather, they reflected on their past histories—some ruefully—and looked to the future with steadfastness.

FINDINGS

As described in Chapter 3, the women in our study lived in a range of settings. Most were single or had never married, although 30 of the women had parented a total of 70 children. Families are the dominant caregivers for individuals with intellectual disabilities worldwide; nonetheless, as people age, they tend to move out of the home (Braddock et al., 2001). This pattern was observed in our study, with women in the oldest age group more likely to live in group homes or institutions.

Health Status

Furthermore, women in this oldest (although smallest) group were more likely to report various health conditions (e.g., in hearing, vision, mobility, and communication) (see Table 8). Focusing on three main conditions likely to influence daily functioning, just one fifth of women overall reported a hearing condition: 10.3% of the youngest group, 28.8% of those 56–70 years old, and 33.3% of the group older than 71 years. Although the prevalence of hearing impairments among adults with intellectual disabilities is high (Evenhuis,

Table 8.   Women reporting health conditions, categorized by age cohort (N = 152)

Age cohort	Hearing	Vision	Mobility	Communication	Disease
40–55	10.3%	41.2%	16.2%	13.2%	16.2%
56–70	28.8	39.4	36.4	12.1	15.2
71+	33.3	61.1	61.1	22.2	27.8

Theunissen, Denkers, Verschuure, & Kemme, 2001), neither individuals themselves nor professional staff members may be aware of these impairments. We cannot say whether the other women in this study did not have difficulties in hearing or whether they had difficulties as yet unidentified.

Nearly one third of the women reported some mobility difficulties (see Table 9), with the oldest group twice as likely as the youngest to do so. Regionally, 37 of the 47 women who reported mobility difficulties were North American and European. Overall, 67 reported a visual impairment (see Table 8).

The health conditions that women reported differed according to where they lived (see Figure 1). Women living with their families were less likely to report vision or hearing difficulties, and just a few of these women stated that they had any medical condition or disease. Not surprising, women living independently were less likely to report mobility difficulties and less likely than women living in group homes or other residential settings to name a medical condition or disease. The pattern of age-related mobility difficulties reflects evidence reported widely that while women in the general population live longer, they may expect to live for more years with functional disabilities (see Figure 2). Overall, 40% of the women who responded said that their health kept them from doing what they wished to do, and this pattern was similar across all age groups. Yet, just 17% of the total said they had an ongoing medical condition or disease, indicating a disparity between reported daily functioning and the presence of a specific, diagnosed condition (see Table 9).

The women who reported an ongoing medical condition referred to a wide array of ailments. Arthritis or other joint pains and seizure disorders were most frequently named. The remaining conditions could mainly be grouped into cardiovascular, endocrinal, skin (e.g., psoriasis, eczema), digestive, and dental problems. Women reported specific conditions such as arthritis, diabetes, cholesterol, thyroid disorders, and mental health difficulties, as well as functional abilities (e.g., "[I] walk slowly with [a] walking stick"). One woman reported "poor memory," and a second, "dementia."

Table 9.   Women who answered "yes" to questions about health conditions ($N = 157$)

Question	Number	Percentage
Do you have an ongoing hearing condition?	33	21.0
Do you have an ongoing communication difficulty?	21	13.5
Do you have any ongoing vital function conditions?	8	5.2
Do you have an ongoing visual impairment?	67	43.2
Do you have ongoing mobility difficulties?	47	30.3
Do you have any ongoing diseases?	27	17.4

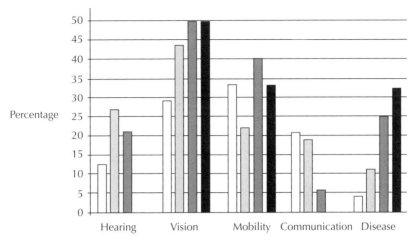

Figure 1.   Women's self-reported health conditions, categorized by residence of women (*N* = 146). (*Key:* ☐ family home, ☐ independent home, ◼ group home, ◼ institution)

Self-Ratings of Health

Nearly two thirds of the women said their health was good, and 80% of women at all ages rated it as excellent or good (see Table 10). These ratings were highly favorable when compared with the general population of older Americans (Merck Insitute of Aging and Health & Gerontological Society of America, 2002), where 42% of the group ages 65–74 reported good or excellent health. When a random sample of Irish women ages 18 years and older were surveyed, 85% of respondents rated their own health as excellent or good (Saffron Initiative Steering Committee, 1999).

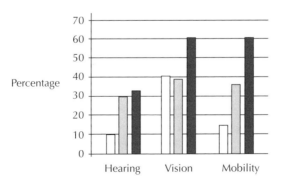

Figure 2.   Percentage of women reporting hearing, vision, and mobility difficulties, categorized by age (*N* = 146). (*Key:* ☐ ages 40–55, ☐ ages 56–70, ◼ ages 71+)

Table 10.   Women's appraisals of their own health

	Percentage	Number
How would you rate your overall health? (*N* = 153)		
Excellent	17.0	26
Good	62.7	96
Poor	16.3	25
Very bad	3.9	6
How would you rate your health compared to others your age? (*N* = 140)		
Excellent	16.4	23
Good	63.6	89
Poor	17.1	24
Very bad	2.9	4
How would you rate your health compared to 5 years ago? (*N* = 140)		
Excellent	11.4	16
Good	59.3	83
Poor	25.7	36
Very bad	3.6	5
Does your health prevent you from doing what you want to do? (*N* = 149)		
Yes	40.3	60
No	58.4	87
Sometimes	1.3	2

In our study, a similar proportion said their health was good or excellent when compared with others of their age, and most women believed their own health now was good, compared with 5 years ago (see Table 10). Taking age into account, most of the women at all ages reported good or excellent health (see Figure 3). Those in the oldest group were more likely to say their health was poor or very bad.

Health Determinants

We asked the women to talk about exercise diet, and sleep—everyday behaviors known to influence health. Three quarters of the women said that they slept well, with the majority going to bed between 8 P.M. and midnight and rising between 5 and 9 A.M. (see Table 11). Two thirds said that they took walks at least once per week, with more than one third doing so every day. It was apparent that North American and European women, especially those in Nordic countries, faced weather constraints in the winter months. One woman liked to walk but did so "not often, but in the summer with the light nights."

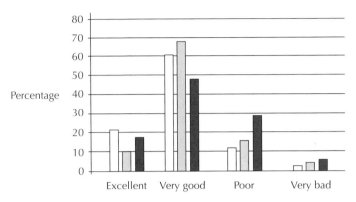

Figure 3. Women's ratings of their own health, categorized by age (*N* = 147). (*Key:* ☐ ages 40–55, ☐ ages 56–70, ■ ages 71–82)

We asked the women whether they regularly took part in any other types of exercise, and 49 women (one third) named one or more particular sports or other forms of exercise:

"Exercises once a week, used to [go] skiing"

"Sometimes swimming, except when it gets cold"

"Swimming, aerobics/arthritis class once a week, tai chi 1 hour on Sundays"

The proportion of women who said they engaged in other forms of exercise was similar across types of living arrangement. However, most women who responded to this question (Question 12 in the Appendix) said they did not do any other type of exercise regularly, with some explaining why: "No, I wouldn't be able to go on exercise things, especially with pedals. My balance won't let me." "I can't do that. My heart won't let me." Others reflected on sports or other forms of exercise they enjoyed but could do no longer: "I used to go skiing, hiking, and fishing." Another group named specific exercises, although some women, it seemed, had adapted the tempo to suit their current situation:

"Yes, bowling one time a week, do exercises at day program every day"

"I take long walks, but I go very slowly"

"Hang clothes on the line, walk to the library"

It was striking that nearly all of the women reported that they ate foods they enjoyed and rated their diet as excellent or good (see Table 11). Just 30% took vitamins.

What the women named as their favorite foods (in response to Question 15 in the Appendix) provided a rich texture with layers of detail. Cultural

Table 11.   Health behaviors

	Percentage	Number
How often do you take walks? (N = 138)		
Daily	38.4	53
3 or more times per week	8.7	12
1–2 times per week	13.8	19
Monthly	1.4	2
Never	7.2	10
Other	30.4	42
Do you do other types of exercise regularly? (N = 149)		
Yes	32.9	49
No	67.1	100
How would you rate your diet? (N = 148)		
Excellent	18.9	28
Good	66.2	98
Poor	11.5	17
Very bad	3.4	5
Do you get to eat foods you enjoy? (N = 150)		
Yes	92.0	138
No	8.0	12
Do you sleep well? (N = 151)		
Yes	77.5	117
No	22.5	34
What time do you usually go to bed? (N = 142)		
6 to 8 PM	9.2	13
8 to 10 PM	57.0	81
10 to 12 midnight	28.2	40
After midnight	5.6	8
What time do you usually get up in the morning? (N = 146)		
Before 5 AM	2.7	4
5 to 7 AM	54.8	80
7 to 9 AM	37.0	54
9 to 11 AM	3.4	5
After 11 AM	2.1	3

notes dominated. North American women described what might be considered as menus from the American heartland, such as "peanut butter and jam on bread, applesauce, meat, vegetables" or "chicken, pork chops, pie, cakes, and ice cream." But other cuisines were described with authority:

"Asado [yellow rice with chicken], empanadas, humitas [corn tamales]"

"Applecake, fish soup, shrimp salad"

"Sushi, noodles, fruits"

"Tortelloni alle erbette [pasta], desserts"

Perhaps in no other testimony did the women's connections with their own cultures emerge in such immediacy and detail. Other women spoke with gusto of the place of food and meals in their lives. Several spoke of flexibility in their food preferences: "I like [eating] every [kind of] food." "[I like] everything."

Besides familiarity with typical foods in their homes and regions, it was also apparent that many women had formed definite views on what they preferred to eat:

"Healthy food, chicken, turkey, drinks with no added sugar"

"Tatties [potatoes] and mince (the only meat I eat). I don't eat meat because of cruelty to animals."

"I do not eat much these days. My favorite is soup."

Another set of comments shed light on living circumstances. One woman said that her husband cooks for her, and she takes whatever he prepares. Therefore, it was hard for her to say she likes it or not. Another woman described losing her appetite and not liking to eat food.

Health Systems

A third category of health indicators related to health systems and more particularly, how the women in our study experienced health care, whether they had regular contact for preventive screenings, and what services they typically used. We asked the women to say whether they took part in routine and preventive health screenings, such as for heart conditions, cervical cancer, or other kinds of cancer. Overall, women were most likely (68.2%) to report general, routine screenings and least likely to have screenings for heart conditions (21%) or cervical cancer (27.4%). Taking place of residence into account, fewer women living with their families had cancer screenings when compared with women living in group homes, where nearly two thirds reported that they did (see Figure 4). By contrast, a similar proportion of women in both settings (about 29%) reported regular screening for cervical cancer.

The women in this study reported an average of three visits to a doctor in the past 3 months, and 1.5 visits to a dentist in the past year (see Table 12). The apparently low level of attention to the possibility of heart disease is striking, given women's increased risk after menopause and the fact that women with intellectual disabilities who have Down syndrome, for example, are likely to experience an earlier menopause (Schupf et al., 1997). Elsewhere, evidence from the United Kingdom suggests that health and social services—although available free of charge—are relatively deficient for elderly people with intellectual disabilities when compared with younger adults (Cooper,

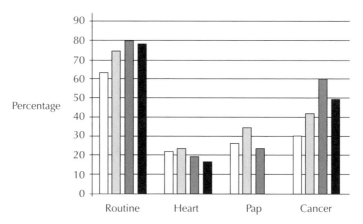

Figure 4.   Women's self-reported access to regular health screenings, categorized by residence. (*Key:* ☐ family home, ▨ independent home, ■ group home, ■ institution)

1997). As evidence indicates, it is likely that multiple factors—including lack of awareness among health professionals of the specific health requirements of older women with intellectual disabilities—contribute to uneven access to health services for this population (van Schrojenstein Lantman-de Valk, Metsemakers, et al., 2002).

Medication

About 14% of the women named specific medications available under prescription, as far as we could judge. A similar group spoke of generic medications such as multivitamins or estrogen. It was striking that many women

Table 12.   Women's responses to questions about health services and systems

	Mean	Range	Number	Percentage
How many times have you seen a doctor in the past 3 months? (N = 123)	3.62	0–90		
How many times have you seen a dentist in the past year? (N = 134)	1.44	0–30		
Positive answer to "Do you take vitamins?" (N = 153)			45	29.4
Positive answer to "Do you have routine preventive health screenings?" (N = 143)			107	74.8
Positive answer to "Do you have routine preventive health screenings (pap)?" (N = 157)			43	27.4
Positive answer to "Do you have routine preventive health screenings (heart disease)?" (N = 151)			33	21.9

knew the purpose of medications, although they did not affix a pharmaceutical label:

"Drugs for high blood pressure, cholesterol, psychiatric treatment"

"Medicine for the muscular skeletal diseases"

"Medicines for digestion, allergy, and nervousness"

Within this group, several women reported that they took unspecified medications for epilepsy, seizures, or "turns," now or in the past: "I used to take something for seizures a long time ago." "Do take med[ication]s but don't know what they are. For seizures."

In summary, our findings revealed a diverse group of relatively healthy middle-age and older women born during the middle decades of the 20th century and further unified as a cohort by administrative labels in their respective countries, setting them apart as having intellectual and associated disabilities. The women reported familiar medical conditions (e.g., arthritis, diabetes, hypertension, epilepsy) and difficulties in mobility or other areas of functioning. They described their ailments in a matter-of-fact tone. Notably, they appraised their own health very positively, even compared with peers. Most said that they could eat, sleep, and exercise as they wished. Some variation in health status and access to care was associated with where the women live and also with their age. Their detailed descriptions of daily activities and preferences shed light on what we have learned about the determinants of health in this population and at the same time provoke important questions to explore.

SUMMARY

What lessons may be learned from the women in this study? First, their accounts refer to the environmental and individual factors that interact to determine health. Some are obvious: daily walks may be out of the question in January in Northern Europe. Women in South America depend almost entirely on family members, not paid residential staff members, to interpret their health needs to professionals. The women in the study reported varying levels of contact with the health systems in their respective countries. It is not apparent whether a particular model best serves women in this population nor whether the availability of universal access to health care in a country guarantees equity and high quality to citizens with intellectual disabilities who seek it.

A second question is whether disparities are evident between health determinants and status of these women and their peers who have physical or other disabilities or older women in the general population in their own countries. More evidence gathered systematically over time will be required in the complex process of closing the gap (U.S. Department of Health and Human Services, 2002).

Finally, an array of questions emerges from women's accounts of their experiences of healthy aging. What personal characteristics are related to mental and physical health? Are some individuals especially resilient or canny in shaping their daily lives? Does the emerging model of self-determination apply equally to women living in such diverse circumstances? For example, diet, exercise, and living and working conditions are key determinants of health. Do women truly exercise choice in deciding what they eat and where and with whom they live? What drives the patterns of nutrition, physical activity, and daily living described by women in this study? What roles do poverty, culture, and family practices play? Understanding how individuals contribute to their own positive health throughout the lifespan is crucial in order to plan strategies for effective health promotion and prevention.

The women who took part in this study had stories to tell about their lives to date in 18 countries varied in culture, climate, economic prosperity, and history of policies related to health and human services. An important theme is health: What features of the environment, society, and the individual intertwine to determine better health of people with intellectual disabilities as they age? We have learned a good deal; even so, many stories are yet untold. Adopting a global perspective casts current knowledge into relief. We know something about the healthy aging of adults in certain, more developed countries documented in sophisticated human service systems. But this knowledge base is swamped by ignorance about the daily lives of millions of men and women with intellectual disabilities silently growing older in homes, villages, streets, and remote countryside in the less developed countries of the world where most people with disabilities live.

CHAPTER SIX

Social Roles

If you think you can grasp me, think again:
my story flows in more than one direction
a delta springing from the riverbed
with its five fingers spread
ADRIENNE RICH

Martha lives in supported housing in a small northern European town. She is 73 years old and, like so many women with intellectual disabilities, has experienced an array of living arrangements throughout her lifetime. She began life living with her parents and two sisters, but when she was very small, she says her mother found it too difficult to care for her, and she was placed in an institution. Although she doesn't remember how long she lived there, she does remember it was a long time and "the staff were no good to me and I was glad to get away from them." She also notes that she had no opportunity for any formal education or employment. She has been living in her current residence for 1 year. Paid care staff help her with bathing, medications, and meals.

Both of Martha's parents are dead, and her sisters live in London. She is impassive when she reports that "London is very far away, so I never see them." Martha does have a son whom she sees every couple of months or so. She doesn't elaborate on that relationship, leaving the impression that it is not close or meaningful for her. She does not offer any particular details about him, such as when he was born or how old he is. Her son does not seem to provide any active emotional or physical caregiving. Martha says that the biggest loss in her life was when her mother died. "When my mother died, I broke down, I phoned my social worker and she helped me. I was looking after my mother for a long time."

Martha is starting to experience the typical health trajectory for older women. She has heart disease, which limits her activities. She reports that she gets dizzy easily and has shortness of breath. She rates her health as poor and says it has been poor for more than 5 years. She does not exercise or take walks, as she worries about her heart. She does see her doctor very frequently but never a dentist. Sleeping is not a problem for her. She goes to bed when she wants and gets up when she wants. Her leisure activities include watching television, listening to music, and going to a lunch club twice each month. She wishes she could do more activities in the community.

Rena is Martha's best and oldest friend. They met in an institution and now live in the same supported housing unit. Rena has the room next to Martha's room. She is the only person whom Martha puts in her inner circle when she is asked to draw a relationship map. John, her son, is a bit further removed from the center of Martha's life than Rena. When recounting a typical day in her life, Martha says, "I watch TV all day. Rena sometimes comes in and sits in the other chair. Rena sometimes comes in here for her dinner. Staff ask me if I want to go to Rena's room for dinner, too." Other entries on Martha's relationship circle illustrate how important paid staff are to her. The second circle out from the center includes her immediate care providers, nurses, advocates, and lunch club friends (people who also have disabilities). The third and most removed circle from Martha includes other paid staff, her foot doctor, her social worker, and her hairdresser.

When asked questions about her well-being, Martha is quick to say that she is happy and the most important thing in her life is to be comfortable. Her paid care providers are reliable and they take care of her basic needs. Once a year, they even take her on a small vacation where they stay in a hotel. She ends the interview by saying, "I don't have any problems, and I don't know what I would want to be different." She returns to her television show and says hello to Rena, who joins her in the next chair.

Women with intellectual disabilities have the potential to participate in all of the same social roles as all other women in society: daughter, sister, aunt, wife, mother, grandmother, lover, friend, confidant, and leisure participant. However, this potential is often truncated or unrealized for many women with intellectual disabilities. In this chapter, we present a review of the literature on social roles for people with disabilities, focusing on family relationships, friendships, and leisure participation. Following the review, we present the findings from our study, including a description of these women's family roles, friendships, role changes, and leisure in the community and at home. The chapter concludes with a discussion of the similarities and differences between the women in our study and the findings in the current literature.

LITERATURE REVIEW

Family Relationships

Despite often erratic living arrangements and early out-of-home placements, Hogg and Moss (1993) projected that family networks provide the bulk of informal support for older people with intellectual disabilities. Blacher (1993) indicated that, in fact, family members are usually the only people with long-term knowledge and contextual memory of family members with disabilities. Professionals, service providers, and friends are too often transient players in the lives of people with disabilities. However, as people with intellectual disabilities age, their contacts with family members become more tenuous, particularly as parent–child connections are lost due to parental aging, disability, and death.

An early study by Seltzer (1985) projected that probably no more than one third of older adults with intellectual disabilities who live in residential settings have contact with their families. This situation is particularly dire when the person's parents are no longer alive and only siblings are left to maintain the family relationships. In a national survey of older adults with intellectual disabilities in New Zealand, Hand (1994) found that approximately 70% of the population had at least occasional contact with their families. Anderson, Lakin, Hill, and Chen (1992) found that among older adults living in congregate community residences, 51% reported that they had no contact with family members. Among this group, half reported that they did not have or did not know about the existence of living family members.

Once parents are gone, siblings are often left to provide support and continuity in the lives of older people with intellectual disabilities. However, as Ashman, Suttie, and Bramley (1993) reported, 30% of people with disabilities do not have siblings. Therefore, family connections pass to extended family members such as aunts, uncles, cousins, nieces, and nephews. As connections move further down the family bloodline, feelings of responsibility and obligation can become more diffuse. In a study of sibling relationships in which one of the siblings was an adult with an intellectual disability, Zetlin (1986) found that types of relationships and interactions ranged widely. The vast majority of siblings had at least some contact with each other. Sisters played a greater role than brothers, and younger siblings were more involved than older siblings. The majority viewed siblings as potential sources for future support, and the adults with disabilities preferred to have some type of reciprocal role in the relationship (e.g., babysitting, giving gifts). As siblings aged, the relationships tended to become more close and reliable.

Griffith and Unger (1994) found that the extent of sibling involvement with a brother or sister with an intellectual disability was dependent on the nature of family relationships and the transfer of parental expectations. Parents who were successful in transferring their concerns and who provided good role models of support tended to have children who fulfilled and often exceeded parents' expectations in supporting family members with disabilities. Bigby (2000b) suggested that siblings play a variety of roles in the lives of older people with intellectual disabilities. She indicated that families who have close long-term relationships tend to have siblings who oversee the well-being of their brothers and sisters, have regular contact with them, and have extensive affective and social contacts with them. By contrast, family relationships that are less close tend to result in less immediate and daily support and intervention between siblings.

Sands and Kozleski (1994) found similar patterns with regard to family roles. In their study, family members were often involved with adults with disabilities in decisions about leisure time and personal space. However, families tended not to include the person with disabilities in decisions about services, living arrangement, care, and financial concerns. In examining how often these adults visited with family and friends, Sands and Kozleski discovered a significant difference in visiting patterns, as compared with the general population. Six percent of the adults with disabilities never visited family or friends, while another 22% only visited them once per month. Ninety-five percent of adults without disabilities reported that they visit family and friends more than twice per week.

Few researchers have examined family relationships and roles from the perspective of second-generation networks and the roles of women with intellectual disabilities as wives and mothers. Such family roles are rarely listed as demographic characteristics of study participants, including major studies on quality of life and life outcomes. It would appear that even among social science researchers, people with intellectual disabilities are not expected to have the opportunity or ability to fulfill such roles. Historically, sterilization policies and images of people with intellectual disabilities as lifelong children negated the possibility that they would have the opportunity to take on such adult responsibilities and reproductive roles. The emerging data that are related to these roles for older people with intellectual disabilities tend to come from population studies in the United Kingdom and former British colonies. Moss and Hogg (1989) in the United Kingdom, Ashman and colleagues (1993) in Australia, and Hand (1994) in New Zealand found that with only a few exceptions, older people with intellectual disabilities have never married and do not have children.

Friendships

People with disabilities tend to develop friendships within very specific contexts, and their friendship circles overall tend to be small. Studying the social interactions of middle-age adults with disabilities who lived in communities in Australia, Ralph and Usher (1995) found that these adults tended to have their most frequent interactions with other people with disabilities. Almost half of the adults who were interviewed reported that they have no interactions with people without disabilities. This finding held true for people with disabilities across prior living arrangements and population areas (i.e., rural, suburban, and urban settings). However, people who had lived in congregate settings prior to the interview tended to have fewer interactions with peers without disabilities.

Examining social integration of older adults with intellectual disabilities who reside in a variety of residential facilities, Anderson and colleagues (1992) found that these individuals have low levels of integration. Only 45% of them reported that they had ever met a neighbor and only 14% said they had visited in the home of a neighbor. Fifty-three percent of older adults who lived in congregate facilities indicated that they had never visited friends or had no friends to visit. Friends tended to be identified only among co-residents. Less than one third of the adults said that they had any contact with people without disabilities who were not their care providers. Social integration, however, was mediated by type of residence, in that people who lived in foster care or group homes were much more likely to have met their neighbors and to have socialized with them.

In a comprehensive study of older adults with intellectual disabilities in Australia, Bigby (1997) found that these individuals tended to have context-specific friendships. Specifically, people tended to have friends only within the confines of their daily activities, such as day activity centers or group homes. Thus, she found that residential mobility and program cessation often left them vulnerable to the loss of significant relationships and friendships. She also found that in social networks, friends tended to provide more incidental affective social supports and contacts rather than direct care or pervasive supports. Harris Interactive (2000) found similar results for people with a range of disabilities. Specifically, 70% of people with disabilities reported that they socialize with close friends, relatives, and neighbors at least once per week. However, this percentage is significantly lower than that of people without disabilities (85%). The percentage gap is even further widened as individuals age, such that older people with disabilities are more isolated than their older peers without disabilities.

Finally, examining the impact of community inclusion on friendships for older adults with intellectual disabilities, Grant, McGrath, and Ramcharan (1995) found that as people moved into community settings or changed settings that friendships were not maintained and that severed long-term friendships with people with disabilities were not replaced by new friends without disabilities. In fact, they found that approximately one third of older adults with intellectual disabilities do not have any friends at all.

Leisure

Given that employment is not a primary activity for older adults with intellectual disabilities, how they fill their days becomes of major importance to them, their families, service providers, and researchers. In a study of older Australians with intellectual disabilities, Ashman and colleagues (1990) found that the situation and life circumstances of people older than 50 were of relatively poor quality, with services and programs designed to meet the needs of groups instead of individuals. Specifically, they found that care providers tended to govern the regularity of access to the community for these older people with intellectual disabilities. In terms of leisure and recreational activities in the community, they found that most activities in adult centers were group oriented. In the home setting, they found that social interactions were basically limited to activities with their housemates or care providers. No individuals in this study reported any friendships outside of their living arrangement. Few people interacted with or even knew their immediate neighbors. By contrast, Hand (1994) found that 60% of older adults with intellectual disabilities in New Zealand participated in leisure activities outside of their residence on a weekly basis. However, care providers indicated that approximately one fifth of the population needed additional activities.

In a quality-of-life study in Colorado, Sands and Kozleski (1994) found that adults with disabilities were less active in their communities than typical adults for many social functions. For example, 67% of typical adults reported that they ate in restaurants one to three times per week, while 41% of adults with disabilities ate out that often. Both groups of adults reported similar patterns of religious service attendance, with 39% reporting weekly attendance, and retail store shopping, with 29% reporting weekly shopping events. Finally, adults with disabilities were more than twice as likely as typical adults to not have visited a bar or tavern in the past year. The adults with disabilities expressed the desire to increase their participation in all of these community functions.

With regard to recreation and leisure participation, Sands and Kozleski (1994) found that adults with disabilities were one third to one half as active as typical adults in such activities as going to the movies, the theater, sporting events, and musical events. When asked if they were satisfied with their level of participation in leisure activities, they tended to desire increased opportunities for participation, particularly in attending movies and sporting events. Mahon and Goatcher (1999) also found that for older adults with disabilities, the likelihood of involvement in recreational activities is considerably less than for typical adults. Nearly half of these adults reported they have no recreational activity and another one quarter stated that they do nothing much.

In a study of program participation for adults older than 65 who lived in a variety of congregate community settings, Lakin, Anderson, Hill, Bruininks, and Wright (1991) found that one third of the adults who lived in group homes participated in day activity centers, and 29% participated in sheltered workshops. Ten percent participated in senior citizen programs, and only 5% were in retirement programs designed for people with developmental disabilities. In addition, the authors found that more than 90% participated in passive leisure activities, such as watching television or listening to the radio. Approximately half of the adults attended community activities, such as the movies or sporting events. Two thirds or more reported that they participated in shopping outings, and more than 80% said they go to restaurants at least once per month. Of particular importance in this study was the finding that while these adults may have been relatively active in a variety of community activities, none of these activities were specifically geared toward the unique needs of older adults. The activities tended to be generic congregate activities in which the seniors could partake if they so desired.

Results from the 2000 Harris Interactive survey of Americans with disabilities found that people with disabilities spend significantly less time outside the home than people without disabilities. This finding held true regardless of age, type, and severity of disability. Older people without disabilities (older than age 45) reported that they went to restaurants, malls, and grocery stores about two times as often as people with disabilities. Fifty-two percent of older adults with disabilities reported that they went to a grocery store at least once per week; 20% said they went to a mall store; and 37% said that they went to a restaurant. These percentages remained the same with people with disabilities who were older than 65 years, as well.

Although the majority of people with disabilities indicated that religious faith was important to them, half of the survey participants indicated that they attend a religious service less than once per month. The lack of attendance appeared to be more associated with physical barriers to such participation rather than the desire of the person with disabilities to participate. With regard to leisure activities, older people with disabilities reported similar patterns of less frequent participation. Only 20% of the older survey respondents said they go to a movie at least four times per year; 7% go to a theater production; 13% go to a sporting event; and 18% go to personal hobby–related events (e.g., stamp show, art show).

Brown, Raphael, and Renwick (1997) studied various aspects of quality of life for people with disabilities in Toronto, Canada. They found that three quarters of people who live independently report that they participate in community events on a daily basis, while half of people living in group homes did so, and only 6% of those in large congregate facilities went out in the community on a daily basis. Approximately 55% of people who lived with family members reported that they go in the community on a daily basis. Cost was a serious barrier to participation for a few people across all types of living arrangements; however, it was a more significant problem for people who lived independently. In terms of using community-based recreation, people who lived in congregate facilities reported that they use community facilities less than once per month, while people living with family or independently reported that they use community facilities at least once per week.

FINDINGS FROM OUR STUDY

Birth Family: Daughter and Sibling

Twenty-five women (16%) reported that they still have one parent alive, usually a mother. With regard to the frequency of seeing their family members, the responses were diverse. The most frequent responses were described as often (38%), which was defined as more than once per week to more than once per month, and rarely (38%), which was defined as less than four times per year, followed by daily (17%). Only eight women (7%) reported that they had no contact with their family members at all. Family contact definitely decreased with age, such that 43.3% of the youngest women, 36.2% of the middle age group of women, and only 20% of the oldest group of women reported that they saw their family members often.

In terms of living arrangements and family contacts, those women who lived in family homes had daily contact with family members. The majority of women who lived independently saw family members often, followed by women who lived in institutions. Women who lived in group homes had the least contact with family members, with 60% reporting rare (less than four times per year) to no contact at all with family members. Finally, in terms of family contact and geographic regions, women in Asia (58%) and Oceania (70%) had the least contact with family members. There are two interesting considerations with regard to the Asian women. One, the majority of these women were married, and yet they did not report frequent contact with their spouses. These women also reported in other parts of the interview that, although they were married, their spouses were often gone from home for extended periods of time to visit their birth families in mainland China. Therefore, these women felt isolated from their marriage partners. Second, many of these women might have interpreted the question to be in reference to their birth families. These women reported that they had little contact with their birth families, and in fact, they reported that they were isolated on farms after their marriages. Finally, in contrast to the Asian and Oceanic women, women in South America had the most frequent contact with their families because most of these women lived with their parents or other immediate family members.

The majority of women responded to an open-ended question on childhood memories. More than half of these respondents (55%) remembered their childhoods as happy, marked by close family relationships and typical lifestyles. An American woman said her childhood was "very happy! I had two brothers and two sisters and my mom and dad." Other women also expressed happy memories:

"We were very close and still are. My sisters watch out for me now."

"I lived with my parents. We were very happy."

"Dad and Mom, they were good. I used to help around the house, do some vegetables and help in the kitchen."

However, many of the women who reported that their childhoods were happy also said that the situation changed dramatically with the loss of a parent or some other family crisis. They indicated that at that point, they were often sent to live with other relatives, but most often they were sent to an institutional setting. As one American woman said, "I got the best care in the world until I turned 13. I was happy as a lark, and then the problems came out. I went to an institution." A Scottish woman's story is particularly poignant in illustrating the precarious fall from family happiness:

> We got on great. Me and my brother used to play. I used to wear his
> boots, and I used to pull him along. We used to smoke my father's
> cigarettes. I was put in [a] home when I was eight. I asked my mother
> why and she said for education and I said, education? I was abused
> there and raped.

Several other women were hesitant to describe their childhoods, as this
woman was: "I don't remember. I was placed at an institution early on, and I
visited my family at holidays or they came to see me. Not often, though. I
don't really want to remember." Often women who were placed in institutions
only saw their birth families a few times each year. A Norwegian woman said,
"I came home to my parents at Christmas and Easter—that's all." Many of the
Norwegian women remembered being children during World War II. They
said things like, "It was bad during the war. It was bad and we had to move
a lot. I was put in an institution. We were poor, and I had to live with an aunt
and then the institution."

Another 36% of the women who responded to the question about their
childhoods only remembered them as unhappy, chaotic, and lonely. They indicated that one or more of their parents was very strict and often abusive. An
Argentine woman's memory was not atypical of this group of women. She said,
"My childhood was very sad. I had a dad, a mom. My dad was an alcoholic and
he punched me everyday. I had six brothers and three half-brothers. They
didn't understand me because of my problem." A Taiwanese woman recalled
that her family did not love her very much because of her intellectual disabilities; thus, she had no status in the family. A Scottish woman experienced the
trauma of broken families and their impact on children with disabilities. She
confided that her childhood was

> [R]eally bad. Mother died when she was having me, and my dad
> remained. When I was three, my stepmother ill-treated me and
> kicked me down the stairs. So the court put me in a mental institu-
> tion. For 25 years, I was ill-treated there too by staff and patients.
> Bad memories.

A final 18% of the women reported that they spent their childhoods in institutions and therefore had no memories of a family life.

When we asked women to reflect on what their family life is like now,
76% of the women responded. Of those women, 57% said that their family
life is currently good and happy. One American woman said her current family relationships are better than in the past because now her difference is more
open and accepted. Her family understands more about the disability. Another

woman who lived in an institution since childhood said her family relationships are

> [B]etter. I'm connecting with my siblings. I didn't have relationships growing up. I have it now. I missed that relationship, but I do like it now. I wish my family life at a younger age would have been different, but I don't regret what happened. It made me stronger and more determined to turn my life around.

The response from a French woman was indicative of how important family relationships were to many of these women:

> I am very close to my family. I often see them. I have many photographs of them. I have a calendar with a very beautiful photograph of my family. My family is close. I am sad when I travel by the bus to return to my program and home, and I leave my family. I am very attached to my family.

Another 43% of the women said that their life is unhappy and that they feel little connection to their families. As one woman from Scotland so poignantly said, "I don't have a family and it brings tears to my sad eyes. I would like to trace them." Another Canadian woman felt the loss of her family. She said, "I'm left on my own now. The staff is my support now."

Family Role Change

More than half of the women (56.4%) reported that they are seeing their role in the family change as they become older. Some of the women indicated that they do not feel as important in the family constellation as they did in the past. Other women were more philosophical, indicating that the aging of the various family members has its natural impacts on them. They receive less help and have less contact with their families. They also noticed that their point of contact within the family was changing with time. A Norwegian woman reflected on the changing roles of family members when she said, "Mamma and pappa are old. I see them less. My sister's children visit me more now."

Women in the youngest age group, 40–55 years old, were most likely to report this role change, with 70% of them noting some change. In looking at role change by living arrangement, women who lived in group homes were the least likely to report that they experienced any changes in their family roles with aging. Only 39% of these women reported any changes. Similar percentages of women in each of the other three living arrangements (i.e., family homes, independent, and institutions) reported that their roles in the family were changing as they aged. More than 60% of these women, in each living arrangement, said there are changes with their own aging. Across all regions of the world, approximately 60% of women reported that they were aware of family role changes with age, with the exception of Oceanic women (in Australia and New Zealand). Just more than one third of the women in this region reported any role changes with age.

Marital Family: Wife, Mother, Grandmother

Although the majority of women in this study were single (87.2%), just under one quarter of these single women had either current significant relationships with a male partner (n = 13) or had been married in the past and were either widowed (n = 7) or divorced (n = 5). The distribution of currently and previously married women is presented in Table 13. Seventeen of the married women indicated that they currently live with their spouses.

Thirty women reported that they have a total of 70 children, and two women reported that they have several grandchildren, though a specific number was not given. The distribution of children for these women by age cohorts and geographic regions is presented in Table 4 (p. 26). Five women indicated that they currently live with one or more of their children. These women's children often serve as sources of financial emotional, and practical support. They own the houses in which the women live and help them with their daily personal care needs. However, the majority of women with children indicated that their children are married and that they have their own children and households. It did not appear from the comments of these women that they saw their children or grandchildren very often. Three women indicated that their children also had disabilities which was a source of worry for them. These offspring lived in group homes or institutions, alienated from their mothers.

Table 13.   Marital status by country

Country	Number currently married	Number previously married
Argentina	1	0
Australia	0	1 widowed
Belgium	2	1 widowed, 1 divorced
Italy	6	1 widowed, 1 divorced
Japan	1	0
New Zealand	2	0
Norway	0	1 divorced
Scotland	0	1 widowed
Taiwan	7	2 widowed
United States	1	1 widowed, 2 divorced
Total	20	12

Friendships

Many of the women reported that they had long-term friendships. Friends were often discussed in terms of childhood and school relationships. These were considered true friends, the gold standard upon which more contemporary friendships were assessed. A Scottish woman said, "Me and Carol have been friends, no matter what." An Italian woman said, "My friendships are better and they are friendships that have lasted many years." Many of the women named one particular friend with whom they had had a long and close relationship. Phrases such as "known her the longest," "his friendship never changes," and "she is my lifelong best friend" were typically used to characterize these stable and important relationships. In terms of intimate relationships, 13 women indicated that they were either dating or living with a partner. Appropriately so, when asked to name the three most important things in their lives, the women who had partners were quick to put their boyfriends first on their lists. One French woman called her partner "my boyfriend, the love of my life." Many of these women had found partners late in their lives, after they had moved out of family homes or institutions. Their partners were their confidants and allies, helping them with problem solving, daily activities, and loss and disappointment.

However, overall, the majority of women in our study rarely mentioned friends without disabilities or who were not part of their small network of relationships. They tended to identify extended family members, friends of family members (as acquaintances), or other people with disabilities when they named their friends. Friends appeared to be most often contextually based, in that the women talked about co-residents and activity center comrades when they were naming their friends. Two Flemish women particularly reflected on the context-specific nature and extent of their friendships. One woman said, "I used to have many friends at work, too. But I can't see them anymore [because she is no longer working]. At school I had some good friends." Another woman said, "When I was still working, I had more friends. But now, as I don't go out a lot, it changed. I do not see the friends [whom] I had at work anymore." An Australian woman had the same observation. She said, "Some friends have changed. I know lots of people who are supported by the same organization but now they live in different areas," from which we infer that she does not see them because of the change in residence. An American woman said, "I don't do things with friends outside of group."

Approximately half of the surveyed women responded to an open-ended question on changes in their friendships over time. Of those women, 64.2% reported that they had perceived changes in their relationships with friends

over time. More than half of the women (65.4%) said the changes were negative. Women tended to report more negative changes in their friendships as
they aged, and many of the reflections on the nature of change in their friendships focused on their aging process. An Argentine woman said, "I had more
friends when I was younger." A Taiwanese woman said she did not have many
new friends and that she had lost contact with her old friend. A Canadian
woman not only thought she had fewer friends, she also was saddened by the
fact that she had few male friends: "I'd like to meet men. I used to have male
friends but now I don't. I don't have as many friends as I used to." Death had
taken some friends away: "Lots of friends have passed away. Used to see my
friends more often." A French woman said, "I do not have any friends. They
all died. I have a friend who took care of my mother, but that was a long time
ago. I no longer see him. They are all dead."

Another common theme on the nature of change in women's friendships
centered on their experiences of living in and subsequently leaving the institution. A woman from Norway said, "I saw lots of people at the institution,
but they weren't friends. Now, I do more things with friends." However, the
feeling that friendships increased after leaving the institution was not universal. One woman said, "I see less people since I left the institution." Another
woman said in response to the question about whether she saw her friends,
"Not much since leaving the institution. You don't see them as much."

For the other 34.5% of the women who said the changes in their friendships were positive, their perceptions were reflective of their positive and
philosophical attitudes toward life. An American woman said, "I'm more at
ease with them now. I don't have to be on guard anymore." A Norwegian
woman said that her life is "much better now that I live with my sister. I have
friends now." A Scottish woman reflected on the impact that a change in her
living situation had on her life, "I've changed since I went to live at Betty's
[in a residential apartment]. I think my friendships are better now." Many of
the women equated the positive changes in their lives with having more
friends and different, more friendly caregivers.

Leisure

At least one quarter of the women indicated that they usually have nothing
to do in their spare time. This percentage held true regardless of the age of
the women or their living arrangement. However, in examining leisure
engagement by geographic regions, we found that nearly half of the women
in North America (42%) indicated that they usually have nothing to do,
while only 6% of the Oceanic women reported a similar circumstance. Next,

we asked the women if their participation in leisure activities outside their home has changed in the past 5 years. Eighty-seven percent of them said their participation has changed. However, interestingly, they were evenly split on the direction of change, with half of the women saying activities have increased and half of them saying activities have decreased. In examining participation by age, we found that the younger women, ages 40–55 years, were more likely to say their activity level had increased, while women older than 55 reported that their activity level had decreased. Not surprisingly, the decrease in activity level was most dramatic for the oldest cohort, women older than 70.

In examining leisure activities in the community, Table 14 presents the range of activities in which the women were engaged, in descending order of frequency of their participation. In addition, the percentage of women who frequently participated in each activity is presented, with *frequently* being defined as more than twice per month. The majority of women reported that their most common leisure activity outside of their home is going to the shopping mall. However, only one quarter of the women who responded to the question on leisure activities in the community indicated that they go to the mall more than twice per month. Those women who do go to the mall indicated that they are most often "window shoppers," tagging along behind their care providers who are there to purchase personal items for themselves. Rarely do these women have enough discretionary money to support desired purchases at the mall. As one woman said,

Table 14. Participation in leisure activities in the community

Activity	Any participation	Frequent participation	
		Subsample	Overall sample
Shop at a mall	73%	23%	17%
Eat at a restaurant	63	24	15
Talk with neighbors	55	61	13
Attend meetings	46	26	11
Visit relatives	44	19	8
Visit friends	39	33	13
Attend religious service	36	5	2
Go to parks	32	14	4
Go to movies	30	6	2
Go to bars	26	7	2
Sporting events	20	10	2
Go to library	17	4	1
Play sports	10	25	3

When our house worker is bored, she decides we should go to the mall. I never have any money to spend, and it's no fun walking behind her while she gets to spend money. I don't like to go to the mall all the time, but I am not allowed to stay home by myself. I wish I had more money to spend so I could buy some yarn for my knitting or some makeup.

The women reported similar experiences in terms of restaurants. They were at the mercy of the desires of their care providers. Most often going to a restaurant for these women meant having a lunch at the counter in a large discount store, in a fast-food restaurant, or in a coffee shop. Very few women went to high-quality restaurants with tablecloths, extensive menus, and professional wait staff.

Talking to their neighbors was the most common social activity in which these women participated. This was the most common activity by age group, geographic region, and living arrangement, with the one exception of women who lived in institutions. This activity was third on their list, which most likely reflects the isolation and severity of disability that is associated with institutional living. In fact, women who lived in institutions did not list visiting friends, relatives, or neighbors at all. Instead, they mentioned going to parks and clubs as their most frequent activities. In further examining leisure activities by geographic regions, we found that European and South American women tended to participate in more social activities (e.g., visiting friends and relatives), while Asian and Oceanic women tended to participate in more outdoor activities (e.g., going to parks, sporting events). After talking with neighbors, North American women ranked going to restaurants and clubs as their next most frequent activities.

Table 15 presents the women's participation rate in various home-based leisure activities. Across all regions of the world, age groups, and living

Table 15. Participation in home-based leisure activities

Activity	Overall sample	Modal frequency
Watching television	87%	Daily
Listening to radio/music	64	Daily
Talking on the telephone	57	Daily
Reading	35	Daily
Sewing	30	Daily
Playing cards	23	Monthly
Doing puzzles	20	Daily
Playing board games	17	Monthly
Gardening	11	Daily
Birdwatching	9	Daily
Playing video games	4	Monthly

arrangements, the vast majority of women indicated that their most common leisure activity is watching television, with more than 85% of the women watching it on a daily basis. However, when we asked the women to name their favorite activity, only six women (6% of the respondents) indicated that watching television was their favorite thing to do. In terms of favorite activities, the women were more likely to name music, bingo, or going to a club as favorite pastimes. Others had particular hobbies, such as pets, karaoke, needlework, and art projects. It is possible that the women represented in our study grew to adulthood in settings in which television formed part of the living environment as a matter of course. In listening to these women paint pictures of a typical day in their lives, we noted that almost all of them indicated that shortly after they rise in the morning, they turn on the television and the last activity of the day is sitting in front of the television. Several women said they wished they did not watch so much television, but it is always there and available. Television seems to function as a passive companion in these women's lives.

In further examining preferences in leisure activities, we found that 63% of the women indicated that they preferred passive activities, while the remaining 37% of the women preferred more active leisure pursuits. There were no real differences in preferences by age group, living arrangement, or geographic region of the world. However, as would be expected, the younger women had a slightly higher preference for active leisure pursuits, while the oldest women preferred to be more passive.

Finally, we asked the women to comment on what changes they would like to make in their activities. A sizeable number of women said that they would not change anything or that they did not know about realistic options or how change would happen. When women did talk about changes they would like to make, they often wished for more friends with whom to do activities, more money with which to pursue activities, improved physical ability to move around their environments, and more opportunities for travel. Dancing was a theme that resounded among the women across all geographic regions. Many of the women said they wished they could go dancing more often. By and large, the women wished they were more active. As one Scottish woman said,

> I would like to do more hill walking again. I really enjoyed that. I enjoyed going places. I would like to swim but I'd need someone with me. I've been to the local baths but they said, "sorry." I think it's because of the way I am and I'd need someone with me.

A Canadian woman said, "I'd like to go snowmobiling, I'd like to do more activities and get more involved with people, socialize more, go out more." A Belgium woman who lives in an institution said,

I would like to go out more often, but then I have to lose some weight first, so that I would not be so tired that fast. Sometimes I see other people going outside and then I would like to go out myself, too.

When we asked the women if they tend to do leisure activities by themselves or with others, just more than half of the women (54.4%) said that they recreate with others. Not surprisingly, the proportion of women who tended to be solitary in their activities increased with age, such that 60% of the youngest group of women reported interactive activities and only 39% of the oldest group of women were interactive. Similar results were found by living arrangement as well, such that women in more congregate settings tended to be more solitary. The majority of women who lived in institutions tended to be solitary in their leisure activities, closely followed by women in group homes. Across all age groups, more than 60% of the women reported that they had a close friend with whom to do activities. Interestingly, in terms of identifying a close friend by living arrangements, an inverse pattern emerged. Eighty-three percent of women who lived in institutions reported having a close friend while only 48% of women who lived in family homes reported having a close friend with whom to do activities. Similarly, women in group homes were more likely to report that they had a close friend with whom to do leisure activities than women who lived independently.

In examining interaction and companionship by geographic regions, we discovered that Oceanic women tended to be more solitary in their leisure activities than women in any other parts of the world. There were no differences in reports of having close friends, in that 50%–65% of the women across all regions of the world said they had at least one close friend with whom to do activities.

Two thirds of the women indicated that they go on vacations, and 77.5% of those women reported that they vacation every year. By age, the oldest women in the study were least likely to go on vacation. The younger women and the older women who did go on vacation reported that they tend to vacation with family members, while the women in the middle age group tend to vacation with friends. The opportunity to take a vacation was differentiated by geographic regions. Only 36% of North American women reported that they were able to take a vacation, followed by 47% of Asian women. By contrast, nearly three quarters of the women in South America, Europe, and Oceania reported that they take yearly vacations. For the women who vacationed, travel destinations and activities are as varied as those of the typical population. They visit distant relatives, go to the sea, visit national parks and historical sites, go to cities, or visit cultural institutions. They also spoke fondly of their vacation experiences, and most women longed for more opportunities for such pleasurable activities. The older women were saddened by the fact that they were not as physically able to travel and that they no longer had family members who would take them on vacations.

SUMMARY

This group of older women with intellectual disabilities was similar and dissimilar from those women presented in other research studies in interesting ways. Most strikingly in terms of family roles, more of the women in our study were married and had children and grandchildren than is often reported in other studies. This finding probably reflects the fact that many of the women in this study had more mild intellectual disabilities than women in other studies. However, it may also reflect cultural differences in expectations and supports for women with intellectual disabilities. For example, the extant literature tends not to include Asian culture and studies. Our study identified that a large number of the Taiwanese women were married and had several children. Perhaps in this culture, marriage is used as a mechanism for ensuring informal supports for the birth family as well as for the woman with an intellectual disability. Similarly, Italian women were the next largest group of married study participants. Again, this finding may reflect sampling bias or different cultural beliefs and behaviors. In either case, the social roles of wife and mother merit further exploration in cross-cultural and aging research in the disability community. It will be particularly interesting to examine these roles for younger women with intellectual disabilities, in light of policy changes, self-determination, and expanded educational and employment opportunities. Such studies may help society to see how far it has truly come toward the widespread implementation of the philosophy of normalization.

In terms of other family relationships, the women in our study showed similar patterns of family engagement and involvement as people with intellectual disabilities in other published studies. Although mothers remained the linchpins in their lives, many women in our study found that siblings were replacing mothers in their daily lives. Typical of all adults caught in their middle age, many of these women were just coming to terms with the loss or impending loss of their parents. On another note, it was very heartening to hear from these women how strong family ties can ultimately be. Many of the women reported that their severed childhood ties were being rekindled as they aged and moved from institutional settings to community living. It was interesting to note that women who lived in group homes seemed to have the least contact with family members. Further research is needed to examine if this reported limited contact is due to personal choice on the part of the woman with intellectual disabilities, the lack of existing family members, or family perceptions that their relative with disabilities is independent and not in need of ongoing family support.

The finding that one third of the women in the study reported unhappy childhoods that were riddled by abuse and loneliness is not surprising, given other studies on violence and abuse among people with disabilities. However, it is disturbing and reflective of the stress and tension that is associated with disability among families who have limited coping skills. This finding also highlights the fact that people with disabilities are not immune to or unaware of their impact on the family. Although the women in our study reported that leaving their birth homes was always a sad event, it often removed a level of stress from their lives. Unfortunately, they most often found new forms of stress and abuse in more institutional settings. Historically, too little research has examined the impact of out-of-home placement on the person with a disability. This study clearly indicates that these women have never forgotten the pain of that childhood separation.

As a whole, these women had small circles of friends. However, the majority of them could name at least one long-term and intimate confidant and friend. In many cases, what was seemingly lacking in quantity was made up for in quality. Consistent with other studies, these women tended to have context-specific friendships with peers who also had disabilities. Friends outside of their immediate networks tended to be family acquaintances and not friends specifically chosen by the woman herself. Most of these women were seeing their networks shrink with age and reduced opportunities for community involvement as a result.

There was a clear sense that residential changes had taken their impact on friendships in these women's lives. They all spoke about losing human connections with each physical move. Even leaving the institution resulted in mixed outcomes for some of these women. A major part of this disruption is due to the difficulties in maintaining contacts and networks without the financial, physical, and emotional supports to do so. These women do not have readily available transportation, network connections such as cellular telephones or e-mail, or in some cases, the skills to create supports that allow them to bridge social divides. Again, future research should examine the impact of residential mobility on the social networks and friendships of people with intellectual disabilities, particularly as those people age.

The leisure life of these women is limited and often not what they would truly desire. Although the women reported that the majority of their leisure activities were passive and solitary in nature, many of them wished that they were more active and interactive. Dancing seemed to be the metaphor they used to symbolize their desired leisure life. Too few women went dancing anymore and wished they could. Television appears to have become the passive mode of choice. Almost all of these women painted a typical day as starting and ending with the television. The television was their companion, a friendly voice in a too-quiet, often lonely residence. The television was always on, but few women indicated that they would choose to watch it. The only community activities in which these women participated on a regular basis were chatting with neighbors, shopping, and going to restaurants. Except for chatting with neighbors, these activities were severely curtailed by their lack of money. These women were often passive observers of others' shopping experiences or sandwich eaters in fast food restaurants. Few of these women reported that they were involved with typical community activities such as age-related social clubs or activity centers. Although aging and disability advocates have been espousing the importance of developing inclusive aging communities for people with intellectual disabilities, there is little evidence that such programs are widely available. Future program development and research seriously needs to address this shortfall in the community inclusion agenda.

In summary, older women with intellectual disabilities have lived half of their lives with mixed results. They all report this is a happy time in their lives, yet they are not without sad memories of less than satisfying childhoods and limited family contacts and friendships. By the quirks of history, policy, and limited expectations, they have not had the opportunity to experience the full breadth of social roles that should be open to them. Some women are just now coming into their own and discovering new avenues of intimacy and family relationships, and for these women, it is never too late. The best is yet to come. For other women, life could have been brighter. Policies and practices need to ensure that serendipity does not dictate the range of human opportunities that women with intellectual disabilities have across cultures and environments.

CHAPTER SEVEN

A Sense of Well-Being

*Be still, mother! Think on the time when
you yourself were three-and-twenty years old—
would you have missed the years you have lived since then?*
SIGRID UNDSET

Sarah, age 60, was very pleased to take part in an interview—she likes nothing so much as a good talk. Since her beloved mother's death some years ago, she has lived very much in the company of women in a single-sex residential center located in rural Ireland. On most weekdays, she travels by private minibus to another building on the campus for day programs, including some contract assembly work and craft activities. She described the move from her family home as the outstanding event in her life in the past 5 years, the boundary between then and now. The circumstances were quite beyond her control: "Well, I suppose coming up here when Mammy got sick and the house was changed for me." It is apparent that changes in home and family life for Sarah and her married sisters are on Sarah's mind a good deal. "When Mammy got sick, then things did change a bit for me but I have to get used to it. Getting used to Mam the way she was and then she died." Since then, Sarah's brother-in-law has been very ill: "He has heart trouble. He is still waiting for a transplant or something."

Currently, Sarah said she has no worries: "No. I was worried a bit when the changes start coming [menopause] but I'm not now. I was told to just let nature take its course. Other than that, I don't have worries." She reckoned that her tenacity is the secret to her life: "Just since I was born, I kept going. I was a jolly child, and I just kept going the best I could. I kept going all my life and I'm still going to this day."

When asked what she thinks when she sees younger women with disabilities today, Sarah reflected:

> Well, that word *disability* can mean different things. Some might be in a wheelchair, some mightn't be able to talk, some might have bad seizures, some could be short on a limb. Well, anyone born with spina bifida could have been in a wheelchair for the rest of their life if they have an operation. They wanted to operate on me, but my father wouldn't let them. He said no. It is hard because you are born with it. I don't know how it happens.

Sarah harbors some dreams: "I would like to get a job for money. Maybe down in a shop, I don't know. I would like to work part-time to try to get a few pounds." Looking ahead 5 years, Sarah said:

> It's hard to know. You wouldn't know whether you'd be in a war with all the business of Iraq. I'd like to see the country the way it was in the olden days. None of this. Well, after the world war, it was peaceful and quiet, and people got on with their lives. Still have my health. If I ever got sick, I'd have to go into a nursing home but while I'm healthy, I'll stay going as best I can.

Until now, we have focused on the strands woven into the lives of the women in our study—their childhood experiences, their health, relationships with family and friends, their work and social status, and their life decisions. In this chapter, we try to grasp the texture of the entire fabric of their lives to date and their reflections on the past and their hopes for the future.

PERSONAL SATISFACTION AND QUALITY OF LIFE

We use the term *well-being* as it connotes the distinctive and irrefutable sense of how well a person feels about how she fares and whether she believes that her interests are served. It overlaps considerably with related terms, such as *quality of life*. In their book for community practitioners in the area of disability, Brown and Brown (2003) reviewed recent definitions of *quality of life* and found that most embraced the concept of *well-being*.

It seemed to us that this aspect of living, too, reflected complex interactions over as many as seven decades. The women depended on and contributed to the places where they lived and the people who make up their personal networks of friends, family members, and professional workers. To understand well-being, then, meant exploring not only each woman's history and prefer-ences but also the context in which she strove for personal satisfaction.

Personal Satisfaction

Caution is advised in applying personal satisfaction as a single measure in appraising well-being, especially when considering the life circumstances of vulnerable people with little power. The very poor, those living in grim resi-dences, or those with sparse opportunities may declare that they are doing well. Perhaps they are merely fulfilling the truth that human beings are noth-ing if not adaptable: "The problem with measuring life satisfaction is that people may simply be making the best of a bad situation and have found ways to compensate" (Brown & Brown, 2003, p. 143).

Many readers might know men and women with intellectual disabilities who have lived or worked in bleak circumstances for years or even decades. Evidence suggests that people with intellectual disabilities tend to express satisfaction with the formal services they use, although not uniformly so. In the United Kingdom, Gregory and colleagues (2001) found that adults with intellectual disabilities varied in the satisfaction they expressed across differ-ent elements of various residential support services, more so with living accommodations and activities and less with friendships, level of risk, and supports received.

Human Strengths

The framework we applied to address the women's well-being reflected core themes of an emerging field of study, positive psychology, which explores what people find worthwhile and satisfying about their lives under normal conditions:

> The field of positive psychology at the subjective level is about val-ued subjective experiences: well-being, contentment, and satisfaction (in the past); hope and optimism (for the future); and flow and hap-piness (in the present). (Seligman & Csikszentmihalyi, 2000, p. 5)

A growing body of evidence has enhanced the field's understanding of factors related to well-being among individuals in the general population. Compara-tively little is known about how to nurture positive traits (e.g., wisdom, resilience) among men and women with intellectual disabilities or even how to identify these positive traits confidently, much less to measure them reliably.

We asked the women in this study to talk about what is important to them, the best and worst events of the recent past, and what they believe to be the secret to their lives. We asked them, too, to look back over their earlier lives to recall past events, mindful that reminiscence serves a particular purpose among older adults by encouraging them to integrate their life experiences and find fresh meaning (Seifert, Hoffnung, & Hoffnung, 1997). We assumed that the same process would serve older people with intellectual disabilities as well. Robert Groulx, a leading self-advocate and President of People First in Montreal, contrasted his current life with earlier years in institutions or marginal employment in this way:

> When I think of my quality of life today, I can say that it is like night and day compared to what it was. I feel that [I] have come out of the darkness. I feel that I have taken my own place in life, and I am happy with the life I live now. Of course I am not rich. . . . I listen to music, and I am happy in my home. (Groulx, Dore, & Dore, 2000, p. 25)

We invited the women to look ahead at their futures, also. By doing so, we aimed to advance a tremendous body of work now in its inception: How can we understand more fully how people with intellectual disabilities gain strength and resilience throughout their adult lives so that they become resourceful on their own behalf?

In this chapter, we present what we learned when we asked the women to reflect on aspects of their well-being. First, we review some of the salient evidence in the burgeoning topic area of quality of life, particularly as this construct encompasses men and women with intellectual disabilities. We describe briefly the quantitative and qualitative measures applied in this study during interviews with women themselves. Next, the findings related to women's well-being in the recent past and the present and their dreams of the future are presented in the context of personal satisfaction and where they live. Finally, we try to draw lessons about what the women believe to have been important for them during their lives thus far, so as to share the wisdom they have gained.

REVIEW OF LITERATURE

In this section, we focus on evidence relating to various aspects of the well-being of people with intellectual disabilities. Key topics selected are definitions of *well-being;* the interplay of personal satisfaction with public domains such as social and political environments; models of quality of life, including the influence of gender and aging; and the importance of self-ratings in measuring life satisfaction.

Well-Being

We adopted a contextual model of well-being, treating it as the product of complex interactions between an individual and nested spheres of influence. Ultimately, each person appraises his or her own life experiences. We were mindful that the women in our study spoke from diverse cultures and personal histories. But for some participants, limited horizons and sparse opportunities to direct their own lives might have led to their positive appraisal of life conditions others would find untenable. It was thus important to acknowledge that—however hard or meager her story seemed—each woman's life was her own to narrate.

Public Policy and Well-Being

The women's stories, of course, did not unfold in isolation, as each woman who took part in the study came to it with a personal history of a life lived in a given time and place. The socioeconomic and political domains cast their shadows for good or ill in terms of public policy with its corresponding impact on service provision. Acting alone, most individuals can do little to alter government decisions or global trends. Although sound, humane policies are necessary in order to put certain conditions in place for citizens, they do not necessarily lead to better outcomes for individuals living in a given country. A cautionary note resonates when public policy focuses on people who are disadvantaged or especially vulnerable in society, such as those with intellectual disabilities. Even if choice is widely valued, it is important to pay particular attention to the well-being of people involved when judging social arrangements and results. An evaluative question might be to what extent do public policies lead to a better, more developed life for individuals? The Nobel Prize–winning economist, Amartya Sen, has discussed the value of social and economic conditions as hard currency with the potential to unlock people's capabilities for development:

> Social and economic factors such as basic education, elementary health care, and secure employment are important not only on their own, but also for the role they can play in giving people the opportunity to approach the world with courage and freedom. (1999, p. 63)

Other mainstream political philosophers have proposed a utilitarian approach to justice based on choices. At the same time, choice has emerged as a driving force in shaping supports for individuals with intellectual or other disabilities. Schalock and Verdugo (2002) noted that choice is a major element in models of quality of life. Other writers have argued that freedom to make choices is the root of this concept (Janicki, 1997), albeit entwined with limits set by income, functional ability, and sparse opportunities.

Quality of Life

Quality of life has a lineage stretching back many centuries, and yet its freshness and utility are perennial. Acknowledging its appeal for researchers and policy makers in many fields, Rogerson (1995) drew parallels between two different conceptualizations of quality of life. The first focuses on the interaction between environmental conditions and personal factors. The second roots quality of life in individual health, and Rogerson suggested that these two approaches have much in common and that each can gain valuable insight from the other. Felce (1997) advocated an integrative approach to defining and applying quality of life and suggested that there is substantial common ground in current conceptualizations. Felce defined *quality of life* as "an overall general well-being that comprises objective descriptors and subjective evaluations of physical, material, social, productive, emotional, and civic well-being all weighted by a personal set of values" (p. 132).

Quality of life is multidimensional, and a substantial overlap with health is a dominant theme. As Schalock and Verdugo (2002) concluded in their detailed review of hundreds of publications on this topic, health and quality of life are close kin. A complex, interactive relationship between the two means that having a good quality of life may lead to better health and vice versa.

Reviewing health indicators literature, Eckermann (2000) indicated that there have been few attempts to develop measures to reflect women's experiences of health, well-being, illness, and disability. Eckermann suggested that a gender approach is vital to capture fully the diversity of men's and women's life experiences and that appropriate indicators should be suited to the level of analysis, whether global, regional, national, special group, or individual.

Quality of Life and Aging

Growing older as a person with intellectual disabilities is, above all, a recently acquired privilege, as the increase in life expectancy in this population has wrought unprecedented changes for individuals, their family members, and society (Ansello & Janicki, 2000). People in developing countries do not expect to live as long as Norwegians or Canadians, for example. In spite of the yawning disparities in life expectancy and other development indicators that separate the rich and poor countries, quality of life has particular appeal. This construct embraces people across cultures and age groups by avoiding traditional categories of disability and focusing on general principles that apply to all (Brown, 2000). Elements of quality of life are weighted and perceived according to the individual's age, circumstances, and culture. Elderly people in the general population are concerned with quality of life: Farquhar (1995) reported that quality of life of people older than 65 in the United Kingdom varied by age—with the very elderly expressing more negative features of the quality of their lives—as well as by region. Health was not the only component. Respondents also valued highly their relationships with family, social contacts, and activities.

In their study of emotional functioning among women older than 65 who have disabilities and were cognitively intact, Penninx and colleagues (1998) used the number of functional living domains affected (e.g., basic self-care) to indicate severity of disability. It was found that a substantial proportion of women in this group could be described as emotionally vital. Their vitality was not alone a function of personal characteristics but also of health status, disability, and sociodemographic context.

Quality of Life and Intellectual Disability

Given the greater longevity and heightened awareness of age-related changes among older people with intellectual disabilities, a good deal more attention has been given to understanding what makes up a life of high quality and to devising suitable applications and measures. To lend cohesion, the debate on how to enhance the quality of life of older people with intellectual disabilities has been grounded in human rights (Herr & Weber, 1999).

Measures of the various components of quality of life should thus reflect the nuances of age and circumstance. For example, choice or autonomy is frequently applauded as the core of conceptualizations of quality of life and, at the level of application, as the gold standard for evaluating human services on behalf of people with disabilities. Distilled to its essence, choice may not be the optimal remedy for older people with intellectual disabilities who have grown to maturity unaccustomed to making choices and who are thus vulnerable to isolation when they are left to their own devices in later life. By contrast, Ansello and Janicki (2000) argued that *assisted autonomy* is preferred, a process involving negotiation and assistance from others that respects the individual's dignity.

Some features of aging embody the human condition and apply to all adults engaged with life transitions in all cultures. As time goes on, older people experience the greater likelihood of death among family members and friends. Adults with intellectual disabilities may be expected to show responses to a bereavement similar to those of all adults—with sadness, anger, anxiety, and pain—and to understand that death is irreversible (Harper & Wadsworth, 1993). Yet their family members or professional workers may not interpret these responses appropriately, especially if the grief-stricken person cannot express herself verbally. Furthermore, individuals with intellectual disabilities in some cultures may even be excluded from funeral rites and rituals (Raji, Hollins, & Drinnan, 2003), thus exacerbating their sense of loss and isolation.

Personal Satisfaction

Although the two concepts are often confused, a country's economic well-being should not be conflated with individuals' well-being and quality of life. Personal well-being is determined at an intimate level of life rather than by broader social conditions (Eckersley, 2000). National standards of living are distinct from subjective measures of quality of life and do not take into account the unique weight an individual may place on aspects of life. For example, having a pet cat or sitting in the sunshine are precious experiences beyond dispute for those who value them. Hence, measures of personal quality of life need not reveal anything about the individual's living conditions or wider society.

Although subjective measures are of crucial importance in appraising quality of life, they must be set in context. Hensel and colleagues (2002) compared people with and without intellectual disabilities on subjective and objective quality-of-life measures. The same high levels of satisfaction were apparent across both groups. Yet, respondents with intellectual disabilities had poorer health and were significantly less satisfied with their health, suggesting that satisfaction alone may not be the most appropriate measure to assess either quality of life or service provision for this population.

Developing reliable measures of personal satisfaction, especially among individuals with intellectual disabilities, is a current endeavor for scholars and practitioners. Examining levels of expressed satisfaction among adults living in a range of settings in the United Kingdom, Gregory and colleagues (2001) found that those living in larger, traditional campus settings expressed more satisfaction with friendships and relationships than those in community-based housing. And groups expressed more satisfaction with accommodation and activities than with friendships and support. Elsewhere, Schwartz and Rabinovitz (2003) found that self-reports of life satisfaction on the part of residents with intellectual disabilities were correlated with those of their parents and staff members. Relationships emerged as a core element in satisfaction. But staff rated more highly the satisfaction of residents who were more able and who lived more independent lives than residents themselves, perhaps illustrating the distinctive benchmarks of these two groups. Schwartz and

Rabinovitz emphasized the importance of including both objective and subjective measures such as well-being in determining quality of life.

In the light of growing consensus that quality of life encompasses choices, the pursuit of happiness, and personal satisfaction, a core dilemma arises: how to balance autonomy and risk? This question exerts a ripple effect when posed about people with intellectual disabilities. Good practice aims to support women with intellectual disabilities, for example, in expressing self-determination and making informed choices about all aspects of their lives—where they live, where they work, and with whom they live and spend leisure time. Yet women in this group across different cultures incur a heightened risk of physical, emotional, and sexual abuse (Walsh & Murphy, 2002).

Self-Ratings

To explore more deeply the roots of personal satisfaction, we may examine what people think is important in their lives. Bowling (1995) focused on health-related quality of life in reporting a survey in the United Kingdom using a generic question about the five most important things in people's lives, in order of priority. The findings indicated that the three most important things were relationships with family or relatives, own health and the health of those close to them, and finance and living standards. The author concluded that the multidimensionality of quality of life should be reflected in attempts to measure this construct.

In summary, we applied a positive, reflective framework encompassing current satisfaction as well as the recent past and the future to explore aspects of the well-being of women in our study. We borrowed themes from quality-of-life models. And we tried to follow the threads of the women's personal narratives through their complex histories as citizens living their lives in particular places and times.

INDICATORS USED

Quantitative Measures

To discern patterns across cultures and age groups, we asked the women to provide information about their personal well-being—whether they felt safe, were sad or happy, felt useful and in control—and what an ordinary day was like for them (see Table 16). These items reflected issues that had emerged in the review of the literature, particularly the themes of present satisfaction contrasted with past experience and future hopes.

Table 16. Women's positive ("yes") answers to questions about specific aspects of their personal well-being

Question	Number answering yes	Percentage responding to question
1. Do you feel safe in your surroundings?	134	90.5
2. Do you feel welcome in your community?	126	90.0
3. Do you often feel pleased about accomplishing something?	128	88.9
4. Are you happy with your living arrangements?	129	88.4
5. Is there someone who cares about how you feel?	128	88.3
6. Have you had to cope with significant life events?	124	87.3
7. Can you make your own decisions?	112	80.6
8. Do you feel useful?	110	79.7
9. Do you feel you have control over your life?	106	76.8
10. Do you get to do what you want to do?	113	76.4
11. Are you interested / excited in something?	110	76.4
12. Do weekends differ from weekdays?	104	71.7
13. Do you have more or less possessions than your friends?	62	52.5
14. Are you worried or anxious during the day?	62	42.2
15. Do you feel sad often?	49	32.9
16. Do you wish you could stay in bed all day?	23	15.6

Qualitative Measures

To elicit the women's experiences of their life histories and conditions and to invite their reflection, we also raised an array of open-ended questions. These also mapped onto main areas of well-being, past, present, and future, but this format allowed the women more scope to reflect on and to tell their life stories. First, to explore current personal well-being, we asked the women to name the three most important things in life, what they believed was the secret of life, and elements of their personal satisfaction and happiness (Questions 14, 24, and 29 in the Well-Being section of the appendix). The women had an opportunity to mention their worries as well. We also asked them to reflect on their lives thus far compared with those unfolding for younger women. Inviting the women to reflect on their past histories, we asked them about what had changed during the past 1–5 years and what were the best and worst things that had happened. Finally, looking to a life as yet unrealized, we asked the women to talk about their dreams and how they foresaw the future 5 years from now.

FINDINGS

In this section, we blend quantitative and qualitative results according to key themes related to the well-being of the women in our study. The findings are presented under three main headings:

- Present personal well-being
- The recent past
- The future

Present Personal Well-Being

Self-reports of overall well-being were obtained using a five-point rating scale ranging from "very happy" (1) to "unhappy" (5). As Table 17 reveals, almost half of the women who responded (48.6%; $n = 71$) described themselves as happy. A similar pattern was observed across the various geographical regions surveyed where the majority of respondents from each region classified themselves as either happy or very happy (see Figure 5).

The pattern of positive reports of well-being extended across age groups. Almost half of the women (48.4%–50.8%) in all age categories (40–55 years, 56–70 years, 71+ years) identified themselves as happy, and a minority in all age categories (3.2%–7.9%) defined themselves as unhappy. Looking at the impact of the women's living arrangements on their state of well-being, we noticed an interesting pattern. Women living in group homes, independent living, or other living arrangements were most likely to classify themselves as happy (ranging from 47.0% to 56.8%), while those residing in their own family home were more likely to define themselves as very happy (40%). The women's general sense of satisfaction with their living arrangements was confirmed by the finding that more than 80% of women in all residential settings (group home, 97.6%; independent living, 84.5%; family home, 84.2%; other residential setting, 86.4%) responded positively to the question "Are you happy with your living arrangement?"

We explored this pattern across various aspects of the women's well-being—whether they felt safe, useful, anxious, that someone cares, or that they could do what they wished to do (see Figure 6). It was apparent that most replied positively, and most often these responses were associated with a professional staff member being named as the most important person in the women's lives.

Table 17. Self-reports of overall well-being ($N = 146$)

	Number	Percentage
Very happy	26	17.8
Happy	71	48.6
So-so	34	23.3
More sad than happy	7	4.8
Unhappy	8	5.5

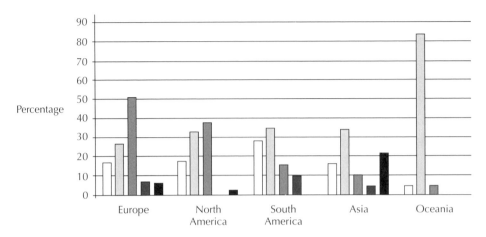

Figure 5. Self-ratings of well-being, by region (*N* = 146). (*Key:* □ very happy, □ happy, ■ so-so, ■ more sad than happy, ■ unhappy)

Of those who answered, 49 women said that they felt sad often, and 32 of these women had named a professional support worker as most important to their well-being. It is worth recalling that less than 20% of all of the women in the study lived with their families (see Chapter 4). We examined the relationship between the women's overall well-being and their primary source of social support. A higher proportion of women whose primary source of support came from agency staff (54.8%; *n* = 40) defined themselves as happy when compared with women whose primary source of support came from a family member (37.8%; *n* = 17).

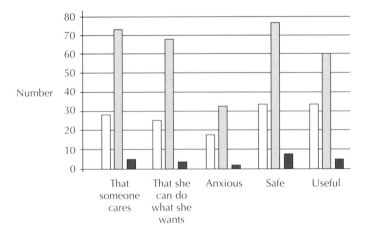

Figure 6. Self-ratings of aspects of well-being, by source of support (*N* = 146). (*Key:* □ family, □ staff, ■ other)

Finally, the relationship between overall well-being and self-reported health was explored. A positive relationship was found ($r = .43$, $p < .001$) with the majority of those who described their health as excellent also describing themselves as happy (56.5%; $n = 13$). In contrast, those who rated their health as very bad said they were more sad than happy (40.0%; $n = 2$).

In addition to an overall self-reporting of well-being, the women were asked to endorse a variety of items relating to specific aspects of their well-being. Their responses are presented in Table 16, which reveals that the over-whelming majority of the women had a positive regard for their surroundings, community and living arrangements (items 1, 2, and 4). The women tended to have less positive regard for aspects of their life concerning autonomy and control (items 7, 8, 9, and 10). Finally, and perhaps unsurprisingly, the women had the least positive endorsement for negative items such as "Do you feel sad often?"

What Are the Three Most Important Things in Your Life?

Many women made general statements about what was important in their lives. Reflecting patterns derived from surveys with the general population (Bowling, 1995), health, home, employment, and financial security were prominent themes: "Happiness—health: your health is your wealth." "To be well everyday." It was evident that many women valued their relationships with both family and friends. The role of each was important, yet distinct: "My boyfriend, my friend, and my parents." "I would like to do more than I do—getting out, I love that it cheers me up, having friends—you can't depend on family."

Religion also played a central role in the lives of some women. One woman said that "belief in God and that He can heal, He can do all things" was most important to her. Another woman put it in a deft summary: "My Lord, my husband, my cat." Indeed several other women named their beloved pets—dogs, cats, and birds—as having a most important place in their lives. Another key area of importance cited by the women was the level of independence they were afforded, as identified by one woman: "Friends, making my own choices, going where I want."

What Are Your Worries?

Nearly one third of the women declared they had no worries, however, as one woman commented, "I try not to worry but trying and saying are two different things." Those who stated that they did have worries commented on various issues including their disability, family members, health, money matters, the future, global threats, and a host of specific dangers and fears. Health was a predominant theme, often intertwined with a second theme—worries about family members who were sources of support: "That I'll get sick and upset and end up in the funny farm again and I'll lose the rest of my family and be left alone."

A major source of worry concerned the women's family members: Fears of death and poor health were frequently cited. Several women interwove fears for their own well-being with that of their family members: "My mother—I am afraid when she dies. I am afraid I will be alone." "[I] worry about my family, how they cope, what will happen to my parents as they get older, and my brother and sisters." One woman had apparently resolved a main worry in her life: "No, [I] used to worry about dying and who would look after Snowy [her pet cat] but now know [two staff members] would [look after her]."

Others expressed worries about their getting along with either family members, friends, or paid support workers:

"Staff yelling at me."

"Sometimes the teachers don't have the time because they have too much to do."

"Worry sometimes about hurting people, hurting their feelings when I don't mean to. I like to be kind to people."

"That I would see my friends forever."

Several global worries reflected current political issues:

"Sitting on boards, I see outcomes of financial things for people with disabilities: funding might get cut. I get frustrated with government and the different ways they want to shuffle the money."

"The Saddam Hussein stuff."

"I heard there may be a war again."

Specific fears revealed a wide array of personal experiences and living circumstances:

"I worry about how I am going to get to places."

"To be rejected by my neighbors; to be robbed."

"I am afraid of darkness."

"I am afraid of crossing streets and roads."

"I am too fat."

Relatively few women mentioned money as a source of worry:

"To lose self-sufficiency and to lose economic security."

"If I have any bills, like my electric bill goes up. I was upset once because the Council [the local housing authority] was going to take me to court for me to license, but my warden did it."

"[N]ot have enough money to live on, like to buy food to eat."

Finally, disability itself emerged as a source of concern for one woman: "My disability, sometimes I wish I wasn't born like this, I wish I was like other people."

What Do You Think Is the Secret to Your Life?

To invite the women to focus on the core of personal well-being, we asked them to identify the secret to their lives. About one quarter did not respond or did not identify any secret. A few women said that they simply relied on religious beliefs: "[I] trust in God to take care of me." Most attributed positive features of their lives to a diverse array of personal and social sources of sustenance, with just one woman mentioning luck. A dominant theme reflected love and affection shared with others:

"When I get upset and I cry, [my friend at the home] gives me a hug and having others who care for me."

"To love my family and friends."

"Talking to my mother and sisters."

"Friends—having people around me and not getting too down by things in my life."

A second major theme was that having a positive attitude, keeping busy, and taking each day one at a time were important in the women's lives.

"To think daily and not to have long-term projects."

"Going out a lot, keeping busy."

"Just since I was born, I kept going. I was a jolly child and I just kept going the best I could. I kept going all my life and I'm still going to this day. I don't think my spine is going to be a problem."

Another group of women mentioned their independence, and other reasons for feeling good about themselves, including good health.

"Living in my own wee house where family and friends can come visit and have a cup of tea."

"I think all the challenges I gave myself and others gave to me.... Because the more people say I couldn't do it, the more I tried and proved everyone wrong. Nobody believed I could garden, and I said I'll show you, and I do it all myself."

"To be content and happy. Not to worry. Does not help to worry or be angry."

"Feeling good about self."

Finally, some women mentioned specific secrets to a contented life, such as securing an apartment, being out of an institution now, even having an opportunity to play bingo. One woman said, "No secret. Hope I have a job and my sons can get married."

When You See Young Girls with Disabilities Today, What Is Different, What Is the Same?

About one third of the women were not sure about how things were different for other women like them today or said there were no differences: "Everything is the same." "Just the same." But another third of the women spoke of greater opportunities, stating that today's girls and women had things easier. Some specifically mentioned more access to employment and education:

"They are allowed to do things I am not permitted to. I would like to use public transportation instead of the sheltered workshop bus."

"We can do nice things but we were not allowed to be principals, nurses, doctors."

"I envy them, their freedom now. When I was young, they cut you off and said you were stupid. I had to fight for the right to go to high school."

"Young women today are more independent economically, and they can decide with more liberty how they spend their free time."

Others made general comments regarding the younger generation:

"They are happier."

"I don't know, but they don't go to institutions any more."

"They're lucky!"

"They don't get put in hospital."

A few women attributed better times to the enviable state of youth or expressed a more tangible sort of difference: "Being young is fun, right. I think that everything is easier when you are young." "They have more friends than me I think."

Empathy for today's girls and women, for many reasons, was striking:

"I feel bad for them because they can't do things themselves."

"Everything is the same as when I was a child."

"I feel sorry for them. I wish there was stuff I could do for 'em but I can't."

"Don't see many of them. They're worse off than me if they don't have their own place."

"I feel sorry for them. I feel there's a future, but not—it's up and down like it was for me. They have the same opportunities as I did. They have to push themselves at something. They can do something and they can make it, like I did."

A few women commented that life is harder now for young women with disabilities:

"I remember being a teenager and having my friends around me and my boyfriends. It's different for girls today 'cause some teenagers think they can throw themselves at boys. I think it's still hard for girls with disabilities."

"They can't do much."

"The ones I know can't go anywhere by themselves."

"It can be a bit harder because times change. It's harder now."

"The last century is different to this. All the crime now."

Some of the women expressed keen awareness of differences, both good and ill, between their own lives and those of younger women:

"I expect them to respect me because I am older. I like when they move forward, I have experience."

"[Women today are] different, aggressive."

"The world is changing. There are more people to know."

The Recent Past

Is Your Day Different From a Day 5 Years Ago?

We asked the women to tell us whether things had changed in the past 5 years. Two thirds (63%) of the women said their typical day was different from the way it was 5 years ago. When the women spoke of these changes, a leading theme was household composition or place of residence. One woman had, for example, "moved from a group home into an apartment. I watch over myself now. I share more. I keep my place clean by myself." Another woman reported that her daily routine was now very different from 5 years ago: "Before I ate at the old people's home, across the street, before I went to the social center on Saturdays." Many women had experienced change for the better in different aspects of their lives: "My attitude—they told me years ago it would be easier and that's true." "My child grow up, and I have grandson and granddaughter."

Not all changes in the previous 5 years were positive. On the contrary, 17 women cited fresh difficulties. Several named functional changes (e.g., hearing and vision), while others said they now found walking problematic. It was striking that lowered ability to walk independently influenced women's lives very distinctively, perhaps reflecting both personal and cultural expectations: "I have more problems hearing and walking. But I have a wheelchair if I need it." By contrast, another woman commented, "I have trouble walking, cannot ski anymore. I miss long hikes." One fifth of the women reflected that nothing had changed over the 5-year period.

What Is the Best and Worst Thing That Has Happened to You in the Past Year?

We asked the women to name the best thing that had happened to them in the past year, and 117 responded. Of these, about one third said nothing or "nothing special" had taken place. One woman was stirred to report that she was "thinking that nothing good happened to [my] life at all."

Pleasant events such as birthday celebrations, vacations, and other gatherings accounted for most of the best memories:

"Celebrating 3 years of working."

"The best time was to have left on holiday with my family."

"I had a beautiful birthday party. All the workers from the sheltered workshop came in."

"Reaching age 65. I made it! And hope to live a long time."

Recent life transitions such as moving to a new home or getting a job were appraised positively:

"Own place, got job, friends."

"I found a boyfriend."

"Working [baking at day program]."

"I am living at group home now."

Remaining responses focused on positive changes that the women identified in their health or functioning: "I have less seizure spells." "Got a wheelchair." Others reported financial gains, such as increased government benefits, new possessions, and strokes of luck:

"New fridge."

"I won my legal hearing [got a settlement]. I was able to pay off my debt and buy things for my kids."

"Won 250 at bingo! Put it in bank book, apart from 30. Will spend it later on clothes."

"To choose my clothes and receive presents."

By contrast, asking women to name the worst thing in the past year revealed a landscape of health difficulties; personal loss; recurring fears of being teased, controlled, or robbed; and a surprising number of falls. About one quarter of the women said that they could not recall such an event or did not know how to respond. Among others, the most frequently named area was the women's own health, and it was evident that these health incidents had been fearful and were recalled in detail:

"Tooth operation with complications, nearly died."

"Having an ear operation—frightening. They put a label around your wrist."

"Hairline fracture of hip."

"Seizure incident—frightening."

"Worst was to have had a cervical smear."

The death of family or friends or the women's own ill health composed the second main area. One woman remarked that the very worst event was All Souls Day, celebrated November 2, when by tradition Catholic families visit graveyards to remember their loved ones with flowers. Many negative events had to do with daily living, at the workplace or at the woman's home. "[T]he changes at the working place." "My work asking me to leave." Some negative events revealed ongoing circumstances that limited personal choices: "My mom and dad stopping me from getting my own place." "Not being able to speak to the others and be ordered around."

Physical injury was a common theme generated by the women with many describing falls, near-accidents, and other incidents that they had found traumatic: "I fell and could not get up. I had to keep lying there until [a friend] came to help me up." "I almost got hit by a car because I was not watching carefully. The man was very angry."

On reflection, many of these negative incidents suggested that the women are aware that they do not direct vast areas of their lives. One woman simply deplored the practice of "moving me around."

The Future

We asked the women to think beyond the moment about two unrealized aspects of their lives: their dreams and their vision of the future in 5 years.

Dreams

Five women did not respond, and a further 28 said they had no dreams. A few said they had relinquished youthful dreams, as they no longer hoped to marry or to bear a child: "Haven't really got any. I used to want to get married, but I don't now I am too old." Dreams reflected different levels, from the global to the personal: "The world—you think it would be a better place...." "To be a little bit smarter, let people understand that I can do things, my family thinks I can't do things, thinks handicapped people can't do anything. I want people to put me at the same level as everyone else."

Enjoyment of life expressed the dream content of a further small group of the women: "To improve my health. To do things that I used to do and can't do any longer, to be able to have more fun." Two women from northern Europe, for example, both of whom were interviewed in January, dreamed of long, bright evenings: "I dream about summer coming." Ten women spoke of dreams specifically related to their future independence:

"Improve my autonomy"

"I shall be living alone [in an apartment]."

"To be in a flat of my own. [I] hope it will come true. I need staff support but I don't think I need to use it."

Another small group dreamed simply that things could continue as they are:

"To continue to live in my house and be independent."

"I'll help with my husband forever."

"Nothing has to change or be added, the way things are is fine."

"I am happy with what I have. I lock my door and watch TV."

A few women spoke about their dreams and hopes for better health: "I would like to lose some weight so that I could go out more often. Now, I sweat and I am tired very soon." For one woman, it seemed that health in the here-

and-now was her priority: "I quit dreaming. I hope I have a better clinical situation."

The women dreamed not only for themselves but also about how their own well-being touched that of family members or friends: "To be closer to my husband and my family; to read and write." "To live with my boyfriend." But sometimes the dream was for a life without family members: "To have my own house without my sisters." Another woman said her dream is that her husband's feet can get better so that he can walk and she can have her own life without taking care of him all the time.

In addition to the many shared dreams described above, more than 40 very personal dreams and ambitions were cited. Travel was a dominant theme:

"Traveling to Buenos Aires and feeling safe."

"I would love to go to Spain again, by plane. I would go for a walk then [with] friends from the day care center."

"My happy dreams are about going on holiday with my mum."

"Travel to America, buy a house in Sardinia."

Marriage and intimate relationships recurred as a second major theme, linked to personal stability and a sense of one's own home: "I dream to have children, to be married. I dream of DB. He knows that I like him. Everyday, I touch his hand."

Concrete goals were wide-ranging:

"I'd like more movies; I'd like to keep my caseworker."

"I have a dream that I would be able to drive, but I know I cannot."

"[I] want to move closer to city center, and I want a new boyfriend. And a dog and a cat."

"[I dream] that I could write letters to [my sister]."

Finally, we asked the women to look ahead 5 years at their future lives. One ruefully predicted that by then she would be "a crotchety old lady." And at least one woman set little store in the future: "I see darkness." About 30 of the women foresaw a future life much the same as the present, although sometimes their predictions were tinged by uncertainty.

"I will be 65 and still much the same."

"Still living here, doing volunteering, things will be different but I don't know how."

"I do not know. I think my son will still live with me. I do not know for sure.

Maybe I will be able to go out more often."

"I'll never be better. I don't think about the future because you never know what's coming forward to you."

Several women focused on their living arrangements when speaking of the future:

"Maybe living in an apartment because I couldn't keep up my house."

"I'll get a new place to live, I know, with a housemate and maybe a cat and a garden and a new boyfriend!"

"Could be that I won't be living here anymore. Maybe I will be living with my boyfriend, and I'll be retired. That is something I would like a lot."

Specific hopes for the future spanned life transitions such as marriage and employment: "[My dream is] that I hope I have something by then, I hope I could get married by then." "I hope I have a job by then."

It was striking that several women reflected on the future in the context of expected changes, although not all were anticipated warmly:

"I can see it, retirement. I would like to be retired."

"I look and see a person that is not me. A person that has changed. I look fatter."

"I see that my husband will retire, and if he stays home all day, we will argue all day. However, we go grocery shopping by car."

"I wait for mail. Cards. The best is to come out to the warm. Cruise, go to Stockholm, get a flight, got to [town] and meet relatives, different trips, visit the town."

"Perhaps I will walk with canes. I will be perhaps stuck in a bed or a wheel-chair. I will be retired but not yet in an old people's home."

These glimpses of the future suggested that the women were steadfast in the face of change. Their voices carried an undertone—that change brings unfore-seen weakness as well as familiar and precious warmth.

SUMMARY

Four fruitful themes emerged from the findings related to the women's well-being. These were correlates of happiness, a sense of missed opportunity, sources of stress and worry, and the mixed blessings of family and friends. Overall, the women in our study said they were happy. Their responses mirrored evidence gathered in other countries and populations. Happiness was associated with the women's living arrangements. A place to live was a theme threading through the women's responses on many other topics. Again and again, women spoke both warmly and warily of their current homes or looked ahead to a better future living in changed circumstances with different people.

Although not startling in themselves, these findings are of great importance to those charged with providing homes for women and men with intellectual disabilities in many countries. Yet they raise a dilemma, too, if the individual's personal satisfaction is mismatched with living conditions that do not meet acceptable standards in her community.

Reflecting profiles of older people in the general population, the happiness of the women in the study was also associated with their sources of social support and self-ratings of health. What they named as the three most important things in life—including health—reflected the ranked values of members of the general population. Responses from several sections converged on the women's awareness of their own health and aspects of healthy aging, lending substance to their potentially valuable contribution to health promotion strategies.

A second theme was rueful in tone. These relatively happy, composed, and long-lived women were nonetheless aware of lost opportunities. Many yearned for marriage and intimacy. A few still desired to bear children, if wryly aware that this was no longer a real option. A strong note was empathy for women like them today, now facing difficult challenges and the disadvantage of living with disability. Yet, personal compassion was blended with their grasp of changed social environments and the awareness that times were different. Many women were mindful that younger women with intellectual disabilities today have a greater chance of living and working where they choose.

Offstage during many interviews, shadows thickened when women referred to various sources of worry, stress, and risk, a third and resonant theme. Insecurity about the future, unstable living arrangements, uncongenial co-residents, and worries about their own or their family members' health were apparent in women's accounts of their lives. It was striking that when asked about the worst event of the recent past, many named fearful events, actual or possible, such as robbery. They documented emotional and physical trauma related to suddenly changed circumstances, some tied to bereavement. The number of falls the women reported was sobering—again, not unexpected given their age range but nonetheless alarming in terms of environmental risk and personal anguish. An ongoing concern reflected that of older caregivers reported very widely elsewhere: If something were to happen to the person who is the primary source of support, what will happen to me? This is indeed the other side of the caregiving coin. The people for whom care is provided have worries about the future in equal measure.

Finally, the women spoke with eloquence and candor about their family members, friends, and professional workers. Undoubtedly, they gained vast stores of solace, affection, and support. It was apparent, too, that they contributed actively to family life and took pleasure in the company of nieces and nephews. But many women chafed against parental control, although the youngest women were older than 40. Some drew a picture of slightly intimidating professional staff members with whom living arrangements were the stuff of daily negotiations. These accounts recalled for listeners that most of the women in our study did not devise their own home and living circumstances in quite the same way that their peers without disabilities did. An uplifting note through many tales involved the daily pleasure and companionship the women found in caring for their beloved pets.

It seemed, then, that these women had achieved considerable satisfaction, mastery, and resilience while retaining a true sense of their own lost opportunities and the pervasive impact of disability on their lives. They had empathy for other women like them and had a degree of well-being tempered by awareness of the benefits and risks of living with other people in a complex, changing world. All things told, we can confidently guess how each would reply to the question posed in Sigrid Undset's heroic novel of a woman's life in 14th-century Norway that appears at the heading of this chapter: *No, I would not have missed one of these years.*

CHAPTER EIGHT

Aging Well

Policy, Practice, and Research Implications

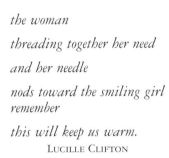

> *the woman*
> *threading together her need*
> *and her needle*
> *nods toward the smiling girl*
> *remember*
> *this will keep us warm.*
> LUCILLE CLIFTON

Rosa is 57 years old, although as she comments, "I don't remember my age because when I was a child I fell down from a chair and this affected my memory." Rosa says that overall she has memory difficulties and these are her main disability. She lives with her family—her brother, brother-in-law, niece, and nephew—in the region of La Plata, near Buenos Aires, Argentina. She lived with her parents and brothers when she was a girl. She attended school, but she is not sure for how many years. Later, she moved on to a sheltered workshop. These days, she works for 30 hours per week in a sheltered workshop, where she sews and earns money for sales of her handiwork. She likes her job.

When asked who are her primary supports, Rosa named her brother, first, and then her brother-in-law. Rosa says that if she had a problem, she would call her brother for help. She does not worry that she might be alone one day: "I have my brother's children. I buy little dolls for them. I love them."

As Rosa spoke more about her daily life at home, it became clear that although her family is close-knit, she nonetheless does her own shopping, laundry, and cooking "because I have to manage myself." Rosa has a daily routine: "I wake up at 7 A.M., and I go to the sheltered workshop. I prepare breakfast before going out. I take the bus." She walks daily and goes to a gym twice each week.

In her leisure time, Rosa also enjoys eating a meal in a restaurant with her family, visiting the homes of her relatives, and shopping from time to time. She named knitting and embroidery as her favorite leisure activities. She says she would like to extend her leisure activities to include "going out, painting, drawing." In addition, Rosa enjoys an annual vacation: "Once a year, with the workers [at the sheltered workshop], we go to the beach." In the past year, Rosa says the best thing that happened were outings: "During the weekends, we go to the woods, eat sandwiches and enjoy the time. I like to go to birthday parties."

Rosa believes that her health is generally good, but currently she complains of "bone troubles" due to past obesity. She rates her diet as good and is especially fond of sweets, honey, ice cream, and salty food such as French fried potatoes. But she does not sleep well. Rosa takes aspirin and vaccinations for flu but no other medications.

The most important things in Rosa's life are her independence and the freedom to use her money as she wants. Rosa also shared some of her worries: "I am afraid of darkness. I wake suddenly up during nights, and I turn the radio on to forget the image of my mother." Of her dreams, Rosa says, "I think about my mother and go to the cemetery to bring her some flowers. This makes me calm."

Rosa believes that today's young girls with disabilities have greater opportunities than she has experienced in her own life to date: "They are allowed to do things I am not permitted to. I would like to use public transportation instead of the sheltered workshop bus." Accounting for the secret of life, Rosa explains:

> I try to be quiet. I think about my destiny when I am alone in my bedroom. I try to forget things from the past. Sometimes my family treats me as if I were a child. They shout at me. I am not used to shouting. When this happens, I feel a cricket in my head.

This chapter presents the summary knowledge from our study. First, it provides a holistic impression of these women's lives, piecing together the common threads in the 167 stories that were told to us. From these stories, we reflect on the resilience and positivism of these remarkable survivors and the unintended impact of storytelling in their lives. Next, we discuss the policy and practice implications and strategies that their stories generate, focusing on the concepts of aging well, self-determination, social networks, stability in their lives, and generic community connections. We end the chapter and thus the book with our reflections on the research implications and haunting questions that these stories generated in us.

WHAT WE HAVE LEARNED

Through this study, we were privileged to have had the opportunity to enter the lives of these 167 older women with intellectual disabilities, who reside in 18 different countries around the world. We assembled the snapshots of their lives to honor their individuality while illustrating the patterns that unite them. The snapshots compose a unique picture, emphasizing that the life of each woman has its own colors and rhythms, and yet there are many similarities among these women. In the following synopsis, we highlight the similarities that weave these women's lives together.

Economic Safety Nets

As a group, these women are poor and have little control over the subsidies that support them and little access to personal money. Almost all of the women are dependent on government and personal subsidies for their subsistence. Members of their support networks make most decisions about their financial resources and needs. Most women worked at some point in their lives, most often in service and assembly jobs with no career orientations. However, their jobs gave them a sense of purpose in the world, and they liked the social interactions that work provided.

Personal Safety Nets

Although all of the women could name key members of their formal and informal support networks, their networks tended to be small and shrinking as the women grew older. The majority of women named a paid care provider as her primary support person. Although the younger women tended to live at home with family members or independently, congregate living increased with age. Overall, the women were satisfied with their living arrangements, and many worried that family or personal health setbacks would disrupt their lives. As the women aged, they tended to rely more on paid caregivers, although they were remarkably independent in their personal grooming and housekeeping activities. As would be expected, independence decreased with age.

Health

As a group, these women were quite healthy, and their perception of their own health was that it was relatively good. They experienced the typical secondary health conditions of aging members of society (e.g., vision problems, decreased mobility). They tended to be quite sedentary and to have less than desirable health behaviors in terms of diet and exercise. They had routine medical care but limited access to preventive screenings and dental care.

Social Roles

Although a large majority of the women were single, 30 women were married and had a total of 70 children. Two women reported that they had grandchildren. Even if family ties were strained or nonexistent, family remained important for these women. Family connections centered them in their worlds, and their mothers provided consistent and lifelong support. Some women reported stressful and traumatic childhoods, riddled by abuse and neglect. Many women were sent to live in institutions at a young age, and they have experienced the evolution of living arrangements brought on by deinstitutionalization policies.

Leisure Time

These women tended to engage in passive, sedentary, and stereotypical leisure activities both in the community and at home. Almost all of the women reported that the television is their constant companion, turned on first thing in the morning and turned off last thing at night. However, few women report that they truly would choose to watch it. They would prefer more active and interactive options, but money and transportation limit their opportunities.

Friendships

Every woman could name one good, longstanding friend. However, their friendship circles tended to be limited to their disability networks and family acquaintances. As the women aged, and therefore had less access to social environments, they found their friendship circles were shrinking. Very few women were involved in generic aging services and programs in their communities.

Well-Being

Overall, these women reported that they were happy, and they had a sense that the best was yet to come. At the same time, they had mixed emotions about loss, sensing that they had missed key normative opportunities in their lives.

They foresaw brighter futures for young women with intellectual disabilities growing up in today's world. They worried about age-related stress and loss but tended to put a philosophical face on it. They had an intuitive sense of the mixed blessings of family and friends, knowing they provided affection and support and yet were at the mercy of their domination. Overall, these women were satisfied with their lives and had developed the resilience to survive and thrive in the face of the many complexities of their societal and personal situations.

REMARKABLE SURVIVORS

To a person, each of these women is a remarkable survivor of a time, a system, and a set of personal circumstances that she did not choose but is living through with dignity and a sense of well-being. Although there are events and situations that in the moment are difficult and stressful for each of these women, they seem to always take the high road and are able to say that this is the best time in their lives and that they live with a hopeful anticipation. These women have learned to survive against amazing odds, and a part of their survival strategy seems to be not to dwell on events over which they do not have control and to always look with optimism toward the future. These women have not forgotten to dream; they have many personal dreams and wishes. What they experience is too few people asking them to share their dreams, and therefore many of their dreams are unrealized, wispy yearnings in the night.

These women appear to have unconsciously developed the very buffers against negative events that are being promoted in the field of positive psychology (Schalock & Verdugo, 2002). They have developed courage, future-mindedness, optimism, faith, hope, honesty, perseverance, and the capacity for flow and insight into their lives and situations. Many of the women talked about painful childhoods, yet they seem to have developed an amazing capacity for forgiveness and have come to terms with the pain and its sources in their lives. They stand as models of how to handle, with dignity and grace, the hand that was dealt to them.

Benefits of Storytelling for the Participants

Although personal narratives and storytelling are important and valued activities in the gerontology field, the disability field is slow in coming to this life-affirming process. Perhaps this delay is the result of just now recognizing that people with disabilities are living into their third and fourth ages, or perhaps it is because we have not looked outside of our own discipline to models of intervention in other fields, or maybe researchers wrongly assumed that we either knew the story or that people with disabilities were not reflective, insightful people. The old adage, if you don't ask, you will never know, could not be more appropriate than in this situation.

After we had completed the interviews, we heard many second-hand stories from our collaborators, service providers, and family members. The unintended impact of our interviews was perhaps the most telling and satisfying part of the entire endeavor. What we heard is that our interviews had been a completely enjoyable process for the participants. They felt important, empowered, and needed. They said that they enjoyed being the center of attention, if only for a few hours. Typically and sadly, they have little opportunity to talk about themselves or to reflect on their lives. It is not a habit or a skill that people with intellectual disabilities are taught, nor is it a skill valued by people in their lives. In addition, our participants very much enjoyed having the undivided attention of the interviewer for an intense period of time. Many participants asked if the interviewer could return in a few months or next year.

Stories of their experiences passed through their residences and their day activity settings, and we would hear from service providers that the younger people with disabilities or their older male peers in those settings were envious of these women's opportunities. The monotony of their daily routines was momentarily broken and for a small time in their lives, the spotlight was shining on them and they were delighted. Many women, in anticipation of their interviews, took extra time in choosing their clothes and makeup the morning of the interviews. It was a date, and they did not want to miss it. During the interviews, many of the women would comment from time to time, "I have never thought about that" or "You really care how I feel about that." They were surprised and enjoyed reflecting and sharing their thoughts on aspects of their lives that they had become socialized not to discuss.

The struggle with which policy makers, practitioners, and families must contend is how to make personal reflection, self-esteem, and one-to-one opportunities a consistent part of these women's lives. These activities and attributes are fundamental components of every person's quality of life, independent of the existence of a disabling characteristic. Personal storytelling should not be a singular experience for older women with intellectual disabilities.

POLICY AND PRACTICE IMPLICATIONS AND STRATEGIES

As a unique group, older people with intellectual disabilities experience fewer choices, less specialized programs, and decreased access to services than their younger peers. These issues are even more poignant for older women with intellectual disabilities because they, like their sisters without disabilities, tend to live longer and in even more relative obscurity than their male counterparts with and without disabilities. Expectations on the part of service providers are limited for these women. They tend to harbor misconceptions about aging and intellectual disability, which are fueled by negative cultural stereotypes associated with age, gender, and disability. Stereotypical phrases such as *triple jeopardy* are popular in the literature. These women have remained hidden from the concerns of policy makers and practitioners who either ignore them or who provide generic services that do not meet their unique needs and interests. In order to create programs and services that celebrate and actualize the golden years for these women, policies and practices must take into account the following concepts and unique characteristics of gender, aging, and intellectual disability.

Aging Well

Successful aging, aging well, and aging in place are all concepts that project the positive spin on growing old that everyone who is moving into retirement years grasps with increasing conviction. The theoretical tenets of successful aging or aging well suggest that older adults continue to have the capacity to live full and interesting lives and that the quality of their lives can be enhanced by focusing on improvements in their environments and activities. Certainly, the stories from the women in this study reflected their ongoing capacity to grow and to thrive, if given the right opportunities, and their desire to grasp a positive philosophy toward aging. Advocates of successful aging promote the following specific principles (Schalock, Devries, & Lebsack, as cited in Herr & Weber, 1999):

- Older adults retain much capacity for growth and development.

- Cognitive interventions can minimize intellectual declines.

- Stimulating and age-friendly environments should be optimized.

- Functioning is enhanced by activity, social and financial supports, and minimal medications.

- Self-determination and personal outcomes should direct service interventions.

These principles undergird an ecological approach to quality of life, which emphasizes the interaction between each person and the larger environment (Schalock & Verdugo, 2002). These principles should direct all services and programs for older women with disabilities, just as they should direct programs for typically aging members of society. In applying these principles to policies and programs, potential promising practices should include

- Active design and advisory boards on programs specializing in services for older people with disabilities. These boards should be composed of the service recipients who can assist in the development and evaluation of the proposed services.
- Program activities that focus on learning, memory, and thinking tasks
- Program environments that encourage a variety of interaction opportunities
- Program activities that facilitate crossgenerational stimulation
- Services that facilitate meaningful involvement with generic community service programs (e.g., Meals on Wheels, hospital volunteers, community gardens)
- Programs that are individualized to the needs and desires of each woman

Self-Determination

Choice and control are key and fundamental indicators of a good quality of life. As part of the human condition, individuals will seek control over whatever choices they are free to make. For the women in our study, often those choices were small and seemingly insignificant (e.g., what radio show to listen to, what to buy with the change in their purses). Family members or care providers frequently made the important decisions in their lives, often without input from the women themselves.

Self-advocates and advocates for people with disabilities are starting to demand that the recipient of services should be directing those services. They demand that the following principles of self-determination underpin all policies and programs for people with disabilities:

- Freedom: The ability for individuals to plan a life, not purchase a program
- Authority: The ability for individuals to control the money to buy desired supports
- Support: The arrangement of resources and people to assist an individual to live a full and satisfying life in the community
- Responsibility: The acceptance of a valued role in the community, including access to employment, home ownership, leisure, spiritual, and other life-enhancing activities (Levitz, 1999)

In applying these principles of self-determination to policies and programs, potential promising practices should include

- Person-directed plans that are free from administrative and family control and intimidation

- Personal budgets with sufficient funds to purchase desired services

- Intergenerational and cross-sectional formal and informal support networks

- Access to work, home of choice, valued community leisure activities, and a variety of life-enhancing opportunities

Social Networks

Although the women in our study all could identify key members of their social networks, overall their networks were small and growing smaller as the women aged. In addition, the networks tended to become more formal with age, so paid care providers became members of the women's inner circles of support as their parents, husbands, or children died or moved on. All of the women in our study emphasized the fact that their exit from employment or changes in residences had disrupted their support networks and friendships. Acquaintances and friends tended to be context bound, such that friends of their parents were their friends by association (although these friendships were rarely maintained if the woman left her family home), and their personal friends were fellow participants or residents in day activity programs or congregate living situations. Friendship development and maintenance is both a skill and an art form, in which people with disabilities are often not intentionally trained; as a result, they lack the ability to extend their informal support networks once losses emerge.

To enhance the social networks of older women with intellectual disabilities, promising practices should

- Facilitate intergenerational networks

- Identify a key network member who will serve as the primary support

- Identify succession lines for the key network member to ensure seamless transitions and sustainable networks

- Facilitate diverse networks so that friendships and supports are not solely disability oriented

- Reduce reliance on formal support providers through creating natural networks with members of the typically aging community (e.g., community friendship schemes, leisure buddy programs, citizen advocacy opportunities) (Bigby, 2000a)

- Create meaningful community activities that will naturally generate new friendships and connections

Stable and Stimulating Living Arrangements

Many of the women in our study had stable living arrangements, but those arrangements were vulnerable to disruption at any time. They did not feel they had control over decisions about their living arrangements, and they knew that their aging process and inevitable need for increased support in their activities of daily living would be the catalysts that started a residential sea change in their lives. The women who lived independently and those who lived in family homes were most concerned, and those women who lived in group homes were most vulnerable to the realities of residential instability. The few women in our study who lived in institutional settings expressed the most satisfaction with their living arrangement, sensing they were not going to be moved and that they had a sense of companionship and support in those settings.

Although physical location and control of the decision to relocate were major concerns for these women, a second very important concern was who was sharing their private space. The women who lived in congregate settings in our study expressed some of their strongest emotions about their housemates and their lack of choice regarding with whom they lived. They often chose self-isolation to escape issues of incompatibility and personal dislike. Their expressed dreams often focused on having the money to live alone or having a place with a friend of their choosing (versus the system assigning someone with whom they had to live). They often had to sacrifice more independent living arrangements for choice of living partners.

Unfortunately, the situation we found is not uncommon in the disability service system. As service systems strive to fit personal needs, policy mandates, and philosophical directions into the realities of inadequate funding, the wishes of the service recipients are too often lost in the squeeze. The rush to address half of the normalization equation (least restrictive living arrangement) runs over the other half of the equation (personal choice and self-determination). Advocates, family members, and service providers must work harder to implement true person-directed planning that acts on the considered and heartfelt desires of these women. No one wants to live in a compromised situation in which even the smallest activities such as taking a drink of water or washing your clothes serve as a constant reminder that you do not want to live with someone who does not wash her glass after using it or steals your clothes from the dryer and then screams when confronted about it.

A second issue in living arrangements for older women with intellectual disabilities is the increasingly smaller circle of stimulation that surrounds their lives. When we asked our participants to recount a day in their lives, the stories were marked by routines that were psychologically, socially, and emotionally understimulated. Television was the one constant in their lives, particularly as they watched their circles of friends shrink and their family ties become more distant and diffuse. Their lack of financial resources and transportation severely limited their opportunities to engage in community activities, so that they increasingly were isolated in their residences. Many of the women commented on the fact that they liked to learn new things or that they wished they were more active.

To enhance the living arrangement for older women with intellectual disabilities, promising practices should include

- Early and intentional discussions about transitions in living arrangements

- Person-directed transition plans

- Transitions to new living arrangements before crisis generates the move

- Personal choice in living partners

- Design of living environments that meet personal needs and desires

- Development of innovative leisure activities that are mentally and socially stimulating

- Inclusion in community service programs as volunteers and workers

Linkage with Generic Service Systems

Very few of the women in this study were involved with generic community services, particularly those that support the unique needs of older people. In fact, current literature indicates that this situation is the norm for older people with disabilities (Bigby, 2000a). Rarely is there any collaboration at the system level or at the individual person level. This lack of collaboration puts older citizens with disabilities at risk of ineffective and inappropriate service provision. As individuals age out of employment, retirement planning should make intentional linkages with the social opportunities and networking services in the aged care services. And when there is emerging collaboration (e.g., as mandated by the U.S. Office of Aging Services), field-based practitioners often see a new source of revenue instead of a requirement to provide unique and expanded services to a new population. Service providers in the aging system rarely are trained in the idiosyncrasies and unique needs of people with lifelong disabilities. Concepts such as person-centered planning, self-determination, and self-advocacy may be poorly understood or devalued by gerontologists when they begin to interact with older people with intellectual disabilities.

To enhance linkages with generic service systems, promising practices should

- Systematically bridge gaps with specialty services

- Support inclusion of people with lifelong disabilities in aging services

- Adapt and resource disability services to support aging in place

- Develop partnerships and collaborative planning to remove systemic barriers

- Provide continuous professional training on collaboration and cross-disciplinary practices

- Fund cross-sector programs at national, state, and local levels to promote inclusionary and seamless services across the lifespan

RESEARCH IMPLICATIONS AND QUESTIONS

As stated in Chapter 3, this study was a glimpse into the lives of older women with intellectual disabilities. It was not designed to distinguish cultural truths about service systems. It was intended to capture themes and to paint a picture of the realities and possibilities in the lives of older women with intellectual disabilities. The themes that have emerged provide the basis for new research directions and questions. Listed below are some questions that continued to haunt us as we compiled these stories.

1. *Would the trends that we observed among these women remain true with a larger, more representative sample?* A carefully and scientifically designed research study would determine if the trends that we found related to demographic characteristics, economic and personal safety nets, health, social roles, and well-being are indeed true for the population of older women with intellectual disabilities. If these trends remain constant across a representative sample, the findings would have interesting and radical implications for policy and service provision for this growing segment of the disability and aging population. Clearly, people with intellectual disabilities are living longer than medical and social science professionals thought was possible. This growing group of service recipients is going to require and demand that the policy and practice field address their unique needs and desires.

2. *How do the lives of younger women with intellectual disabilities compare with these older women in relation to demographic characteristics, economic and personal safety nets, health, social roles, and well-being? What role does society*

and culture play in determining the lifestyle of younger women with intellectual disabilities? Our study was somewhat retrospective; it would be interesting to examine the lives of younger women, particularly to design a longitudinal study that would follow women across the decades of their lives. When we asked our study participants to reflect on opportunities for younger women, they had mixed reactions. Some women thought not much had changed, others thought the younger women had more freedoms and opportunities. A research study that examined the impacts of policy initiatives and philosophical principles, such as self-advocacy and self-determination, on younger women with intellectual disabilities would be very informative to families, advocates, and service providers.

3. *What is the impact of societal values and culture on lifestyle among women with intellectual disabilities?* Again, although not representative, our study did reveal differences in cultural patterns among the women whom we interviewed. For example, the majority of Taiwanese women who were interviewed were married. This may have been a convenient sample and not at all representative of Taiwanese women with intellectual disabilities, but their very existence made us wonder about the societal values and culture that supported and encouraged marriage among women with intellectual disabilities. We wondered if marriage was used in societies where formal support structures were less prevalent as a mechanism to ensure that these women had a built-in informal support structure. The women who were married in Taiwan tended to live in rural settings where they were essential contributors to the agrarian lifestyle. Would marriage be as prevalent in more urbanized settings and societies? We observed similar patterns among the Italian women who were interviewed. Again, was this a sampling bias or a true phenomenon? How were marriage decisions made? Did the women have free will and choice or did families arrange these marriages? Were the marriages established for romantic reasons or were there other more pressing considerations? A well-designed qualitative study could contribute valuable insights into these social roles.

4. *How would older women with intellectual disabilities rate themselves on self-determination indicators? How would their ratings compare with young women with intellectual disabilities, men with intellectual disabilities, and same-age women in the typical population?* From this line of inquiry, we could start to understand where the gaps are in these women's lives. The findings could help to direct policy makers and service providers in creating pro-

grams and services that truly support self-determined lives for older women with intellectual disabilities. This question would be particularly interesting to examine cross-culturally and within the context of the realities of women's living arrangements, employment opportunities, and social networks.

5. *What is the nature and quality of the relationship between mothers with intellectual disabilities and their children? Do intergenerational supports exist, and if so, what is the nature of those supports?* Our study revealed that 30 of the 167 women had a total of 70 children, but it was beyond the scope of our study to examine more in-depth dimensions of these mother–child relationships. Further research should address the nature of the mother–child relationships, the characteristics of the children, the experience of parenting on the part of these women, and the relationship between the women and their adult children and grandchildren. A good qualitative study could examine these relationships through intense interviews with each mother–child dyad. A wealth of questions could be addressed examining such areas as choice making, decision making, parenting skills, parenting supports, roles and role reversals, quality of interactions, and parent and child hopes and dreams.

6. *What is the ideal support system for mothers with intellectual disabilities who are raising their own children?* We have heard from self-advocates that many of them want and have children, yet they feel particularly vulnerable to the threat of court-sanctioned removal of their children. They have strongly indicated that they want to be good parents but often lack the skills or good role models for how to handle the daily demands of parenting. Instead of court removal of their children, they want training in parenting skills and helpful support programs. We need to know more about how to appropriately and helpfully support women with intellectual disabilities who are raising children. We need to identify models of support that facilitate mothers' self-esteem and skills while stimulating the optimum normative development of their children.

7. *How can the prevalence of abuse and violence be diminished in the lives of women with intellectual disabilities?* Many of the women in our study talked painfully about the abuse that they suffered as children and about the stress and trauma that that abuse had caused in their lives. Some women, more than 30 years later, could talk about the lasting effects of the childhood abuse in their lives. Although models of training programs for people with intellectual disabilities related to abuse and violence are emerging, more research is needed to understand how to sup-

port families to prevent the occurrence of violence and how to support girls and women in protecting themselves from abuse.

8. *What is the nature and quality of the lives of women with intellectual disabilities who live in countries with emerging economies? How are these women similar and different from those of women with intellectual disabilities who live in countries with highly developed economies?* When we began this study, we had hoped to address this question with some detail. However, we encountered several barriers in attempting to obtain data from collaborators in countries with emerging economies. Among the barriers were difficulties in distance communication systems, difficulty for collaborators to ascertain a sample of women in their countries, difficulty with cultural attitudes and mores about disability, difficulty in translation of many variables in terms of culture and economics, and difficulty in meeting timelines. It seems that such a study would require extensive resources in terms of personnel, money, and infrastructure supports to be successful. Working with and under the auspices of an international body, such as the World Health Organization or the World Bank, would perhaps provide the authority and infrastructure to address the many issues that such a study would encounter. Among other variables, such a study could address parameters such as the women's opportunities and roles in emerging economies and their formal and informal sources of support and resilience. An intended outcome of such a study would be to learn how to best support women with intellectual disabilities who live in emerging economies to have the opportunities to lead self-sufficient and self-determined lives.

9. *How can formal and informal support providers assist people with intellectual disabilities to develop the necessary buffers against negative events in their lives? Said another way, how do we foster resilience in the lives of people with intellectual disabilities?* The field of positive psychology asserts that people who are able to develop buffers (e.g., futures orientation, optimism, faith, perseverance, capacity for flow and insight) against negative events in their lives will have more satisfying and higher quality lives. Given that people with intellectual disabilities are particularly vulnerable to a variety of negative events, support providers need to either minimize the events or develop strategies for assisting people in moving forward in their lives. An in-depth qualitative study of the markers of successful buffering would illuminate this line of inquiry.

10. *How do we create supportive environments and ideal support networks that allow older people with intellectual disabilities to age well and to age in place? What*

are the necessary characteristics of those environments and networks? Aging is not the end of a productive life but merely a new phase in it. Certainly, the women in our study were excited about what still lay ahead for them and yet they were anxious about their support networks, living arrangements, and personal health. Further research is needed to examine supportive structures that facilitate successful aging for older people with intellectual disabilities.

11. *How do we foster valued roles for older people with intellectual disabilities in the larger community?* Many of the women in our study indicated that their support circles were diminishing and that they had nothing important to do during the day. Few of the women were involved in meaningful employment, and watching television was their one universal, though undesired, activity. Yet, these women clearly had a great capacity to make a valued contribution to their communities. They could be active volunteers in any number of community service programs and typical senior programs. We need research on successful models of valued community inclusion for older people with intellectual disabilities. A second level of research should focus on successful training and dissemination programs that create skilled and committed service providers who will facilitate sustainable models of community inclusion.

12. *What other life-enrichment activities do older women and men with intellectual disabilities desire, and how do we facilitate them?* This question goes hand-in-hand with the previous one, but it is intended to address activities that go beyond community service options. One third of the women in our study said they have nothing to do in their lives—whether in the employment or leisure domains. Many other women said they were at the mercy of their care providers for leisure activities, and as a result some women found themselves doing things that were not truly of interest to them but rather were of interest to their care providers (e.g., going to a bar, shopping for clothes and makeup, going to a fast-food restaurant). We need a better understanding of what activities would be satisfying and life-enhancing for women and men with intellectual disabilities as they age. Are their interests similar to or different from their peers without disabilities? Are there models in the typical aging community that could be adapted to the needs and interests of this population?

13. *How do the lives of older men with intellectual disabilities compare with the lives of these women in relation to demographic characteristics, economic and personal safety nets, health, social roles, and well-being?* As we gathered our stories from older women, we often heard men expressing their interest in tell-

ing their stories. It would be very interesting to see the similarities and differences between older men and women and to see how the same policies and practices were differentially applied and experienced by the two groups. As with this current study and those that have been proposed, a study focusing on men would illuminate gaps in the service system and activities that may contribute to satisfying and self-determined lives for them.

14. *How can some of the specific life-affirming activities from the field of gerontology be successfully incorporated into the lives of older people with intellectual disabilities, such as storytelling, creating personal narratives, and creative expression?* The women in our study delighted in telling their stories and we had the clear impression that they had much more to tell than we could capture in a 3-hour interview. We had created a spark that needed ongoing nurturance to come to self-satisfying fruition. Further research is needed to identify successful strategies for adapting activities from the field of gerontology to the interests and learning styles of older people with intellectual disabilities. Day programs could benefit from such ideas and staff could benefit from training that is targeted to helping them develop and implement such activities.

SUMMARY

And so we have come full circle in capturing the various aspects of these women's lives. To paraphrase poet Lucille Clifton, we have tried to thread together the women's needs and the needle, to the future benefit of all women with intellectual disabilities. We have attempted to give a voice to the quiet world of older women with intellectual disabilities. Across the world, they are living their lives in quiet dignity, believing for the most part that the best is always just ahead of them. We hope these stories will help policy makers and practitioners to assess their views about older people with disabilities. Now is the time to create systems and services that truly address the needs and desires of our aging citizens with disabilities. We also hope these stories have provided a new level of insight for family members. Women with intellectual disabilities do not want only to be cared for. They also want to be cared about, a sentiment that is often lost in the rush to fulfill good intentions. We again thank the women who have allowed us to glimpse into their lives and to recount their stories. They welcomed us with unconditional trust, and they believed that we would tie their threads together. We hope that this book will make a difference in their lives.

References

Addis, M.E., & Mahalik, J.R. (2003). Men, masculinity, and the contexts of help seeking. *American Psychologist, 58,* 5–14.

Altman, B.M. (1996). Causes, risks, and consequences of disability among women. In D.M. Krotoski, M.A. Nosek, & M.A. Turk (Eds.), *Women with physical disabilities: Achieving and maintaining health and well-being* (pp. 35–56). Baltimore: Paul H. Brookes Publishing Co.

Alvarez, J. (1999). *Reflections on an age quake.* New York: United Nations.

Anderson, D.J., Gill, C., & Brown, L. (2000). *Women aging with mental retardation and developmental disabilities.* Chicago: Rehabilitation Research and Training Center on Aging and Mental Retardation, University of Illinios.

Anderson, D.J., Lakin, K., Hill, B., & Chen, T. (1992). Social integration of older persons with mental retardation in residential facilities. *American Journal on Mental Retardation, 96,* 488–501.

Ansello, E.F., & Janicki, M.P. (2000). The aging of nations. In M.P. Janicki & E.F. Ansello (Eds.), *Community support for aging adults with lifelong disabilities* (pp. 3–18). Baltimore: Paul. H. Brookes Publishing Co.

Ashman, A., Hulme, D., & Suttie, J. (1990). The life circumstances of aged people with an intellectual disability. *Australia and New Zealand Journal of Developmental Disabilities, 16,* 335–347.

Ashman, A., Suttie, J., & Bramley, J. (1993). *Older Australians with an intellectual disability. A report to the Department of Health, Housing and Community Services Research and Development Grant Committee.* Queensland: The University of Queensland.

Austen, J. (1992). *Persuasion.* New York: Everyman's Library. (Original work published 1818)

Beange H. (2002). Epidemiological issues. In V.P. Prasher & M.P. Janicki (Eds.), *Physical health of adults with intellectual disabilities* (pp. 1–20). Oxford: Blackwell Publishing.

Berthoud, R., Lakey, J., & McKay, S. (1993). *The economic problems of disabled people.* London: Policy Studies Institute.

Bierman, A.S., & Clancy, C.M. (2001). Health disparities among older women: Identifying opportunities to improve quality of care and optimize functional health outcomes. *Journal of the American Medical Women's Association, 56,* 155–160.

Bigby, C. (1997). In place of parents: The sibling relationships of older people with intellectual disabilities. *Journal of Gerontological Social Work, 29,* 3–21.

Bigby, C. (2000a). Informal support networks of older adults. In M.P. Janicki & E.F. Ansello (Eds.), *Community supports for aging adults with lifelong disabilities* (pp. 55–70). Baltimore: Paul H. Brookes Publishing Co.

Bigby, C. (2000b). *Moving on without parents: Planning, transitions and sources of support for middle-aged and older adults with intellectual disability.* Baltimore: Paul H. Brookes Publishing Co.

Blacher, J. (1993). Siblings and out-of-home placement. In Z. Stoneman & P. Waldman Berman (Eds.), *The effects of mental retardation, disability, and illness on sibling relationships: Research issues and challenges* (pp. 117–141). Baltimore: Paul H. Brookes Publishing Co.

Bowling, A. (1995). What things are important in people's lives? A survey of the public's judgements to inform scales of health related quality of life. *Social Science and Medicine, 41,* 1447–1462.

Braddock, D. (Ed.). (2002). *Disability at the dawn of the 21st century and the state of the states.* Washington, DC: American Association on Mental Retardation.

Braddock, D., Emerson, E., Felce, D., & Stancliffe, R.J. (2001). Living circumstances of children and adults with mental retardation or developmental disabilities in the United States, Canada, England and Wales and Australia. *Mental Retardation and Developmental Disabilities Research Reviews, 7,* 115–121.

Brown, I., & Brown, R.I. (2003). *Quality of life and disabiilty: An approach for community practitioners.* London: Jessica Kingsley.

Brown, I., Raphael, D., & Renwick, R. (1997). *Quality of life: Dream or reality? Life for people with developmental disabilities in Ontario.* Toronto: Centre for Health Promotion, University of Toronto.

Brown, R. (2000). Learning from quality-of-life models. In M.P. Janicki & E.F. Ansello (Eds.), *Community supports for aging adults with lifelong disabilities* (pp. 19–40). Baltimore: Paul H. Brookes Publishing Co.

Bulmer, M. (1987). *The social bias of community care.* London: Allen & Unwin.

Burt, D.B., Loveland, K.A., Chen, Y.-W., Chuang, A., Lewis, K.R., & Cherry, L. (1995). Aging in adults with down syndrome: Report from a longitudinal study. *American Journal on Mental Retardation, 100,* 262–270.

Clifton, L. (2000). *Blessing the boats.* Rochester, NY: BOA Editions.

Cobbs, E.L., & Ralapati, A.N. (1998). Health of older women. Women's health issues: Part I. *Medical Clinics of North America, 82,* 127–144.

Cooper, S-A. (1997). Deficient health and social services for elderly people with learning disabilities. *Journal of Intellectual Disability Research, 41,* 331–338.

Crewe, N.M., & Clarke, N. (1996). Stress and women with disabilities. In D.M. Krotoski, M.A. Nosek, & M.A. Turk (Eds.), *Women with physical disabilities: Achieving and maintaining health and well-being* (pp. 193–202). Baltimore: Paul H. Brookes Publishing Co.

Dalley, G. (1988). *Ideologies of caring: Rethinking community and collectivism.* Basingstroke, UK: Macmillan.

Davidson, P.W., Prasher, V.P., & Janicki, M.P. (Eds.). (2003). *Mental health, intellectual disabilities, and the aging process.* Oxford: Blackwell Publishing.

Doren, B., & Benz, M. (2001). Gender equity issues in the vocational and transition services and employment outcomes experienced by young women with disabilities. In H. Rousso & M. Wehmeyer (Eds.), *Double jeopardy: Addressing gender issues in special education* (pp. 289–312). Albany: State University of New York Press.

Eagly, A.H., & Wood, W. (1999). The origins of sex differences in human behavior: Evolved dispositions versus social roles. *American Psychologist, 54,* 408–423.

ECHI Project Working Group. (2001). *Design for a set of European community health indicators. Final report.* Luxembourg: European Commission, Health Monitoring Program.

Eckermann, L. (2000). Gendering indicators of health and well-being: Is quality of life gender neutral? *Social Indicators Research, 52,* 29–54.

Eckersley, R. (2000). The state and fate of nations: Implications of subjective measures of personal and social quality of life. *Social Indicators Research, 52,* 3–27.

Evenhuis, H.M., Theunissen, M., Denkers, I., Verschuure, H., & Kemme, H. (2001). Prevalence of visual and hearing impairment in a Dutch institutionalized population with intellectual disability. *Journal of Intellectual Disability Research, 45*(5), 457–464.

Fairchild, S.R. (2002). Women with disabilities: The long road to equality. *Journal of Human Behavior in the Social Environment, 6,* 13–28.

Farquhar, M. (1995). Elderly people's definitions of quality of life. *Social Science and Medicine, 41,* 1439–1446.

Felce, D. (1997). Defining and applying the concept of quality of life. *Journal of Intellectual Disability Research, 41*(2), 126–135.

Fujiura, G.T. (2002, December). *Key trends affecting disability health and policy.* Paper presented at the Tampa Scientific Conference on Intellectual Disability, Aging, and Health, University of South Florida, Tampa.

Fujiura, G.T., & Yamaki, K. (1997). An analysis of ethnic variations in developmental disability: Prevalence and household economic status. *Mental Retardation, 35,* 286–294.

Fujiura, G.T., & Yamaki, K. (2000). Trends in demography of childhood poverty and disability. *Exceptional Children, 66,* 187–199.

Gill, C.J., & Brown, A.A. (2000). Overview of health issues of older women with intellectual disabilities. *Physical & Occupational Therapy in Geriatrics, 18*(1), 23–36.

Gill, C.J., & Brown, A.A. (2002). Health and aging issues for women in their own voices. In P.N. Walsh & T. Heller (Eds.), *Health of women with intellectual disabilities* (pp. 139–153). Oxford: Blackwell Publishing.

Grant, C., McGrath, M., & Ramcharan, P. (1995). Community inclusion of older adults with learning disabilities. Care in place. *International Journal of Network and Community, 2*(1), 29–44.

Gregory, N., Robertson, J., Kessissoglou, S., Emerson, E., & Hatton, C. (2001). Factors associated with expressed satisfaction among people with intellectual disability receiving residential supports. *Journal of Intellectual Disability Research, 45,* 279–291.

Griffith, D., & Unger, D. (1994). Views about planning for the future among parents and siblings of adults with mental retardation. *Family Relations, 43,* 221–227.

Groce, N.E. (1997). Women with disabilities in the developing world. *Journal of Disability Policy Studies, 8,* 177–193.

Groulx, R., Dore, R., & Dore, L. (2000). My quality of life as I see it. In K.D. Keith & R.L. Schalock (Eds.), *Cross-cultural perspectives on quality of life* (pp. 23–27). Washington, DC: American Association on Mental Retardation.

Hand, J. (1994). Report of a national survey of older people with lifelong intellectual handicaps in New Zealand. *Journal of Intellectual Disability Research, 38,* 275–287.

Hanna, W.J., & Rogovsky, B. (1991). Women with disabilities: Two handicaps plus. *Disability, Handicap and Society, 6,* 49–63.

Harper, D.C., & Wadsworth, J.S. (1993). Grief in adults with mental retardation: Preliminary findings. *Research in Developmental Disabilities, 14,* 313–330.

Harris Interactive. (2000). *2000 N.O.D./Harris survey of Americans with disabilities.* New York: Author.

Heller, T., & Factor, A.R. (1993). Support systems, well-being, and placement decision-making among older parents and their adult children with developmental disabilities. In E. Sutton, A.R. Factor, T. Heller, B.A. Hawkins, & G.B. Seltzer (Eds.), *Older adults with developmental disabilities: Optimizing choice and change* (pp. 95–106). Baltimore: Paul H. Brookes Publishing Co.

Heller, T., & Marks, B. (2002). Health promotion and women. In P.N. Walsh & T. Heller (Eds.), *Health of women with intellectual disabilities* (pp. 170–189). Oxford, UK: Blackwell Publishing.

Hensel, E., Rose, J., Stenfert Kroese, B., & Banks-Smith, J. (2002). Subjective judgements of quality of life: A comparison study between people with intellectual disability and those without disability. *Journal of Intellectual Disability Research, 46,* 95–107.

Herr, S.S., & Weber, G. (Eds.). (1999). *Aging, rights, and quality of life: Prospects for older people with developmental disabilities.* Baltimore: Paul H. Brookes Publishing Co.

Hogg, J., & Moss, S. (1993). The characteristics of older people with intellectual disabilities in England. In N. Bray (Ed.), *International review of research in mental retardation: Vol. 19* (pp. 71–92). New York: Academic Press.

Hooyman, N. (1983). Social support networks in services to the elderly. In J.K. Whittaker, J. Garbarino, & Associates (Eds.), *Social support networks: Informal helping in the human services* (pp. 133–164). Hawthorne, NY: Aldine.

Horowitz, S.M., Kerker, B.D., Owens, P.L., & Zigler, E. (2000). *The health status and needs of individuals with mental retardation.* New Haven, CT: Department of Epidemiology and Public Health, Yale University School of Medicine & Department of Psychology, Yale University.

Ingstad, B., & Whyte, S.R. (Eds.). (1995). *Disability and culture.* Berkeley: University of California Press.

Janicki, M.P. (1997). Quality of life for older persons with mental retardation. In R.L. Schalock (Ed.), *Quality of life: Vol. 2. Application for persons with disabilities.* Washington, DC: American Association on Mental Retardation.

Janicki, M.P., & Ansello, E.F. (Eds.). (2000). *Community supports for aging adults with lifelong disabilities.* Baltimore: Paul H. Brookes Publishing Co.

Janicki, M.P., Dalton, A.J., Henderson, C.M., & Davidson, P.W. (1999). Mortality and morbidity among older adults with intellectual disability: Health services considerations. *Disability and Rehabilitation, 21,* 284–294.

Keith, K., & Schalock, R. (Eds.). (2000). *Cross-cultural perspectives on quality of life.* Washington, DC: American Association on Mental Retardation.

Kerr, M.P. (1998). Primary health care and health gain for people with an intellectual disability. *Tizard Learning Disability Review, 3,* 6–14.

Kerr, M.P. (2002). Men's health: The female of the species is more healthy than the male. In P.N. Walsh & T. Heller (Eds.), *Health of women with intellectual disabilities* (pp. 219–227). Oxford, UK: Blackwell Publishing.

Krauss, M.W., Seltzer, M.M., & Goodman, S.J. (1992). Social support networks of adults with mental retardation who live at home. *American Journal on Mental Retardation, 96*(4), 432–441.

Lakin, K., Anderson, S., Hill, B., Bruininks, R., & Wright, E. (1991). Programs and services received by older persons with mental retardation. *Mental Retardation, 29,* 65–74.

Land, H. (1995). Rewarding care: A challenge for welfare states. In P. Saunders & S. Shaver (Eds.), *Social policy and challenges of social change: Proceedings of the National Social Policiy Conference* (pp. 1–24). Sydney: Social Policy Research Centre.

Laplante, M.P., & Carlson, D. (1996). *Disability in the United States: Prevalence and causes, 1992. Disability Statistics Report* (7). Washington, DC: U.S. Department of Education, National Institute on Disability and Rehabilitation Research. (ERIC Document Reproduction Service No. ED 400 635)

Larson, S., Larkin, C., Anderson, L., & Kwak, N. (2001). Demographic characteristics of persons with mental retardation/developmental disabilities living in their own homes or with family members: NHIS-D Analyses. *Mental Retardation/Developmental Disability Data Brief, 3*(2), 1–15.

Lee, S., Sills, M., & Oh, G. (2002). *Disabilities among children and mothers in low-income families.* Syracuse, NY: Institute for Women's Policy Research, Syracuse University.

LeRoy, B.L., Evans, P., & DeLuca, M. (2000). *United States and European school-aged disability prevalence: An investigative study to elaborate differences.* Paris: Organisation for Economic Co-operation and Development.

LeRoy, B.L., & Kulik, N. (2002). *A Michigan application of the OECD resource model of special needs education.* Paris: Organisation for Economic Co-operation and Development.

Levitz, M. (1999). Self-advocacy for a good life in our older years. In S.S. Herr & G. Weber (Eds.), *Aging, rights, and quality of life: Prospects for older people with developmental disabilities* (pp. 279–287). Baltimore: Paul H. Brookes Publishing Co.

Lindeboom, M., Portrait, F., & van den Berg, G.J. (2001). *An econometric analysis of the mental-health effects of major events in the life of elderly individuals.* Bonn: IZA, Discussion Paper 398. (Available from IZA, P.O. Box 7240, D-53072, Bonn, Germany, iza@iza.org)

Lunsky, Y., & Havercamp, S. (2002). Women's mental health. In P.N. Walsh & T. Heller (Eds.), *Health of women with intellectual disabilities* (pp. 59–75). Oxford: Blackwell Publishing.

Mahon, M.J., & Goatcher, S. (1999). Later life planning for older adults with mental disabilities: A field experiment. *Mental Retardation, 37,* 371–382.

Matthews, S., Manor, O., & Power, C. (1999). Social inequalities in health: Are there gender differences? *Social Science & Medicine, 48,* 49–60.

McNeil, J.M. (1997). *Americans with disabilities: 1994–95. Current Population Reports, P70-61.* Washington, DC: U.S. Department of Commerce, U.S. Government Printing Office.

Merck Insitute of Aging and Health & Gerontological Society of America. (2002). *The state of aging and health in America.* Available on-line at http://www.miahonline.org/resources/reports/

Messent, P.R., & Cooke, C.B. (1998). Physical activity, exercise and health of adults with mild and moderate learning disabilities. *British Journal of Learning Disabilities, 25,* 17–22.

Moss, S., & Hogg, J. (1989). A cluster analysis of support networks of older people with severe intellectual impairment. *Australia and New Zealand Journal of Developmental Disabilities, 15,* 169–188.

Mulvany, F., & Barron, S. (2003). *Annual report 2002: National intellectual disability database committee.* (Available from Health Research Board, 73 Lower Baggot Street, Dublin 2, Ireland.)

Mulvany, F., & Mulcahy, M. (2002). *Changing profile of the population with intellectual disability in the Republic of Ireland.* Paper presented at the Inaugural Conference of IASSID Europe, University College Dublin, Ireland.

Murphy, E.M. (2003). Being born female is dangerous for your health. *American Psychologist, 58,* 205–210.

Newacheck, P.W., & Halfon, N. (1998). Prevalence and impact of disabling chronic conditions in childhood. *American Journal of Public Health, 88,* 610–617.

Oakes, J.M., & Rossi, P.H. (2003). The measurement of SES in health research: Current practice and steps toward a new approach. *Social Science and Medicine, 56,* 769–784.

Park, J., Turnbull, A.P., & Turnbull, H. R. (2002). Impacts of poverty on quality of life in families of children with disabilities. *Exceptional Children, 68*(2), 151–170.

Patja, K., Molsa, P., Iivanainen, M., & Vesala, H. (2001). Cause-specific mortality of people with intellectual disability in a population-based 35-year follow-up study. *Journal of Intellectual Diability Research, 45,* 30–40.

Penninx, B.W.J.H., Guralnik, J.M., Simonsick, E.M., Kasper, J.D., Ferrucci, L., & Fried, L.P. (1998). Emotional vitality among disabled older women: The women's health and aging study. *Journal of the American Gerontological Society, 46,* 807–815.

Perleth, M., Jakubowski, E., & Busse, R. (2001). What is "best practice" in health care: State of the art and perspectives in improving the effectiveness and efficiency of the European health care systems. *Health Policy, 56,* 235–250.

Pope, S.K., Sowers, M., Welch, G.W., & Albrecht, G., (2001). Functional limitations in women at midlife: The role of health conditions, behavioral and environmental factors. *Women's Health Issues, 11,* 494–502.

Porrell, F.W., & Miltiades, H.B. (2002). Regional differences in functional status among the aged. *Social Science & Medicine, 54,* 1181–1198.

Prasher, V.P., & Janicki, M.P. (2002). *Physical health of adults with intellectual disabilities.* Oxford, UK: Blackwell Publishing.

Raji, O., Hollins, S., & Drinnan, A. (2003). How far are people with learning disabilities involved in funeral rites? *British Journal of Learning Disabilities, 31,* 42–45.

Ralph, A., & Usher, E. (1995). Social interactions of persons with developmental disabilities living independently in the community. *Research in Developmental Disabilities, 16,* 149–163.

Rich, A. (1989). *Time's power: Poems 1985–1988.* New York: W.W. Norton.

Robertson, J., Emerson, E., Gregory, N., Hatton, C., Turner, S., Kessissoglov, S., & Hallam, A. (2000). Lifestyle-related risk factors for poor health in residential settings for people with intellectual disabilities. *Research in Developmental Disabilities, 21,* 469–486.

Robine, J.-M., Romieu, I., & Cambois, E. (1999). Health expectancy indicators. *Bulletin of the World Health Organization, 77,* 181–185.

Rogerson, R.J. (1995). Environmental and health-related quality of life: Conceptual and methodological similarities. *Social Science and Medicine, 41,* 1373–1382.

Rowe, J.W., & Kahn, R.L. (1998). *Successful aging.* New York: Pantheon Books.

Saffron Initiative Steering Committee. (1999). *The Saffron report on women's lifetime health needs.* Dublin, IR: Author.

Sands, D.J., & Kozleski, E.B. (1994, June). Quality of life differences between adults with and without disabilities. *Education and Training in Mental Retardation and Developmental Disabilities,* 90–101.

Schalock, R., & Verdugo, M.A.V. (2002). *Handbook on quality of life for human service practitioners.* Washington, DC: American Association on Mental Retardation.

Schupf, N., Zigman, W., Kapell, D., Lee, J., Kline, J., & Levin, B. (1997). Early menopause in women with Down syndrome. *Journal of Intellectual Disability Research, 41,* 264–267.

Schwartz, C., & Rabinovitz, S. (2003). Life satisfaction of people with intellectual disability living in community residences: perceptions of the residents, their parents and staff members. *Journal of Intellectual Disability Research, 47,* 75–84.

Seelman, K., & Sweeney, S. (1995). The changing universe of disability. *American Rehabilitation, 21,* 2–13.

Seifert, K.L., Hoffnung, R.J., & Hoffnung, M. (1997). *Lifespan development.* Boston: Houghton Mifflin.

Seligman, M.E.P., & Csikszentmihalyi, M. (2000). Positive psychology: An introduction. *American Psychologist, 55,* 5–14.

Seltzer, M. (1985). Informal supports for aging mentally retarded persons. *American Journal of Mental Retardation, 90,* 259–265.

Seltzer, M., & Krauss, M. (1994). Aging parents with co-resident adult children. The impact of lifelong caring. In M. Seltzer, M. Krauss, & M. Janicki (Eds.), *Lifecourse perspectives on adulthood and old age* (pp. 3–18). Washington, DC: American Association on Mental Retardation.

Sen, A. (1999). *Development as freedom.* Oxford, UK: Oxford University Press.

Sherman, A. (1994). *Wasting America's future: The children's defense fund report on the costs of child poverty.* Boston: Beacon Press.

Singh-Manoux, A., Adler, N.E., & Marmot, M.G. (2002). Subjective social status: Its determinants and its association with measures of ill-health in the Whitehall II Study. *Social Science & Medicine, 56,* 1321–1333.

Siperstein, G., Norrins, J., Corbin, S., & Shriver, T. (2003). *Multinational study of attitudes toward individuals with intellectual disabilities: General findings and calls to action.* (Available from Special Olympics, 1325 G Street, N.W., Suite 500, Washington, DC 20005)

Slee, R. (1996). Disability, class and poverty: School structures and policing identities. In C. Christensen & F. Rizvi (Eds.), *Disability and dilemmas of education and justice* (pp. 96–118). Philadephia: Open University Press.

Sonnander, K., & Claesson, M. (1999). Predictors of developmental delay at 18 months and later school achievement problems. *Developmental Medicine and Child Neurology, 41*(3), 195–202.

Stalker, K., & Harris, P. (1998). The exercise of choice by adults with intellectual disabilities: A selected literature review. *Journal of Applied Research in Intellectual Disabilities, 11,* 60–76.

Starfield, B., & Shi, L., (2002). Policy relevant determinants of health: An international perspective. *Health Policy, 60,* 201–218.

Stavrakaki, C. (1999). Depression, anxiety and adjustment disorders in people with developmental disabilities. In N. Bouras (Ed.), *Psychiatric and behavioural disorders in developmental disabilities and mental retardation* (pp. 175–187). Cambridge, UK: Cambridge University Press.

Stiker, H. (1997). *A history of disability* (W. Sayers, Trans.). Ann Arbor: University of Michigan Press.

Sweeney, E. (2001). *Preserving the safety net: Maintaining services for those with barriers to work.* Washington, DC: The Urban Institute.

Sweeney, E. (2002). *Update on what we know about people with disabilities and TANF.* Washington, DC: The Urban Institute.

Szalda-Petree, A., Seekins, T., & Innis, B. (1999). *Women with disabilities: Employment, income and health.* Missoula: Research and Training Center on Rural Rehabilitation, University of Montana.

Taylor, T. (1997). *The cultural competence exchange. National center for cultural competence newsletter.* Washington, DC: Maternal and Child Health Bureau, Health Resources and Services Administration, U.S. Department of Health and Human Services, Public Health Service.

The Economist. (2002). *Pocket world in figures: 2003.* London: Profile Books.

Thorpe, L., Davidson, P., & Janicki, M. (2001). Healthy ageing. Adults with Intellectual disabilities: Biobehavioural issues. *Journal of Applied Research in Intellectual Disability 14,* 218–228.

Tøssebro, J., Gustavsson, A., & Dyrendahl, G. (Eds.). (1996). *Intellectual disabilities in the Nordic welfare states: Policies and everyday life.* Kristiansand, Norway: Høyskoleforlaget.

Traci, M.A., Szalda-Petree, A., & Seninger, S. (1999). *Turnover of personal assistants and the incidence of injury among adults with developmental disabilities.* Missoula: Center on Rural Rehabilitation Services, University of Montana.

Trent, J.W. (1994). *Inventing the feeble mind: A history of mental retardation in the United States.* Berkeley: University of California Press.

Turner, S., & Hatton, C. (1998). Working with communities: Health promotion. In E. Emerson, C. Hatton, J. Bromley, & A. Caine (Eds.), *Clinical psychology and people with intellectual disability.* London: John Wiley.

Turner, S., & Moss, S. (1996). The health needs of adults with learning disabilities and health of the nation strategy. *Journal of Intellectual Disability Research, 40,* 438–450.

Turnham, H., & Dawson, S.L. (2003). *Michigan's care gap: Our emerging direct-care workforce crisis.* New York: Paraprofessional Healthcare Institute.

U.S. Department of Health and Human Services. (2002). *Closing the gap: A national blueprint to improve the health of persons with mental retardation. Report of the Surgeon General's Conference on Health Disparities and Mental Retardation.* Rockville, MD: Office of the Surgeon General.

Undset, S. (1930). *Kristin Lavransdatter* (C. Archer & J.S. Scott, Trans.). London: Alfred A. Knopf. (Original work published 1922)

United Nations. (1994). *Standard rules on the equalization of opportunitites for people with disabilities.* New York: Author.

United Nations. (1997). *Women's rights: The responsibility of all. Basic information kit No. 2.* New York: Author.

United Nations Development Programme. (1999). *Human development report 1999.* New York: Oxford University Press.

United Nations Development Programme. (2002). *Human development report 2002.* New York: Oxford University Press.

van Schrojenstein Lantman-de Valk, H.M.J. (1998). *Health problems in people with intellectual disability.* Maastricht, Netherlands: Proefschrift Universiteit Maastricht.

van Schrojenstein Lantman-de Valk, H.M.J., Metsemakers, J.F.M., Haveman, M.J., & Crebolder, H.F.J.M. (2002). Health problems in people with intellectual disability in general practice: A comparative study. *Family Practice, 17,* 405–407.

van Schrojenstein Lantman-de Valk, H.M.J., Schupf, N., & Patja, K. (2002). Reproductive and physical health. In P.N. Walsh & T. Heller (Eds.), *Health of women with intellectual disabilities* (pp. 22–40). Oxford: Blackwell Publishing.

Walsh, P.N. (2002). Women's health: A contextual approach. In P.N. Walsh & T. Heller (Eds.), *Health of women with intellectual disabilities* (pp. 7–21). Oxford, UK: Blackwell Publishing.

Walsh, P.N., & Heller, T. (Eds.). (2002). *Health of women with intellectual disabilities.* Oxford, UK: Blackwell Publishing.

Walsh, P.N., Heller, T., Schupf, N., & van Schrojenstein Lantman-de Valk, H.M.J. (2001). Healthy ageing—Adults with intellectual disabilities: Women's health and related issues. *Journal of Applied Research in Intellectual Disabilities, 14,* 195–217.

Walsh, P.N., Kerr, M.P., & van Schrojenstein Lantman-de Valk, H.M.J. (2003). Health indicators for people with intellectual disabilities: A European perspective. *European Journal of Public Health, 13*(Suppl. 3), 47–50.

Walsh, P.N., & Murphy, G.H. (2002). Risk and vulnerability: Dilemmas for women. In P.N. Walsh & T. Heller (Eds.), *Health of women with intellectual disabilities* (pp. 154–169). Oxford, UK: Blackwell Publishing.

Waters, E., & Doyle, J. (2003). Evidence-based public health: Cochrane update. *Journal of Public Health Medicine, 25,* 72–75.

Wehmeyer, M. (1996). Essential characteristics of self-determined behavior of individuals with mental retardation. *American Journal on Mental Retardation, 100,* 632–642.

Wolfensohn, J.D. (2002, December 3). Poor, disabled and shut out. *The Washington Post*, A25.

World Health Organization. (1998). *The world health report 1998. Life in the 21st century: A vision for all.* Geneva: Author.

World Health Organization. (2000). *Ageing and intellectual disabilities. Improving longevity and promoting healthy ageing: Summative report.* Geneva: Author.

World Health Organization. (2002). *The world health report 2001. Mental health: New understanding, new hope.* Geneva: Author.

Zehnder-Merrell, J. (2001). *Kids count in Michigan. Data book 2001: County profiles of child well-being.* Lansing: Michigan League for Human Services.

Zetlin, A. (1986). Mentally retarded adults and their siblings. *American Journal of Mental Retardation, 91,* 217–225.

APPENDIX

Interview Protocol

Section I: Demographics

1. What is your birthday? _____
   month/day/year

2. How old are you? _____
   years

3. What is your racial/ethnic background?

4. What is your marriage or significant relationship status?

   ☐ Single ☐ Never married ☐ Dating

   ☐ Married ☐ Widowed ☐ Living with
   significant other

   ☐ Separated/divorced

5. What is your major disability?

6. What town/community do you live in? _____
   town/state/country

7. Do you have any children? If yes, how many?

8. How many people live with you?

9. What is their relationship to you?

---

10. Where do you live?

☐ Family home   ☐ Group home
☐ Apartment   ☐ Institution
☐ Own home   ☐ Other: _____

11. If you live in your own home/apartment, do you rent it or own it?

12. How long have you lived in this place? _____
                                              years

13. Did you receive any formal education? If yes, how many years?

14. What type of school was it?

15. Did you ever, or do you now, work for money? If yes, how many hours per week did/do you work?

16. What kind of work did/do you do?

17. Do you like it?

18. What is the *best* thing about your job?

19. What is the *worst* thing about your job?

Section II: Economic and Personal Safety Nets

1. Who provides your primary support? What is his/her relationship to you? Who is the most important to you in terms of support (mark with an asterisk)?

2. How much time per day does [person named in Question 1] help you?

3. Would you say that [person named in Question 1] is very reliable?

4. Do you ever worry that you will be alone, without the help you need? Please explain.

5. Is [person named in Question 1] easily available? Please relate some stories.

6. How close is [person named in Question 1] to your home?

7. What are your sources of economic support? (Please list.)

8. What is your annual income?

9. Do you manage your own money?

10. Do you do your own shopping (groceries, personal items, clothing, etc.)?

11. How do you travel in the community?

☐ Walk   ☐ Private car (of a friend, a neighbor, or a relative)
☐ Bus   ☐ Own car (drive yourself)
☐ Taxi   ☐ Other: _____

12. Do you make your own meals?

13. Do you do your own housework?

14. Do you do your own laundry?

15. If you could change anything about your economic and personal support systems, what would you do?

Section III: Health

1. How would you rate your overall health?
   ☐ Excellent   ☐ Good   ☐ Poor   ☐ Very Bad

2. How would you rate your health compared with others your age?
   ☐ Excellent   ☐ Good   ☐ Poor   ☐ Very Bad

3. How would you rate it compared with 5 years ago?
   ☐ Excellent   ☐ Good   ☐ Poor   ☐ Very Bad

4. Does your health prevent you from doing what you want to do?

5. How many times have you seen a *doctor* in the past 3 months?

6. How many times have you seen a *dentist* in the past year?

7. What medications do you take regularly? (Please list.)

8. Do you take vitamins?

9. Do you have any ongoing medical conditions?

    ☐ Hearing   ☐ Mobility   ☐ Communication
    ☐ Vision   ☐ Vital functions   ☐ Diseases (e.g., diabetes)
    ☐ Other: _____

10. Do you have routine preventive health screenings? If yes, please check:

    ☐ Pap   ☐ Cancer (e.g., breast, colon)   ☐ Heart disease

11. How often do you take walks?

12. Do you do other types of exercise regularly? If yes, what and how often?

13. How would you rate your diet?

    ☐ Excellent   ☐ Good   ☐ Poor   ☐ Very Bad

14. Do you get to eat foods you enjoy?

15. What are your favorite foods? (Please list.)

16. Do you sleep well?

17. What time do you usually go to bed?

18. What time do you usually get up in the morning?

Section IV: Social Roles

1. Tell me about your family.

2. How often do you see your family?

3. What was your family life like when you were a child?

4. What is your family life like now?

5. Tell me about your friends.
    Who?
    How long have you known the person?
    How often do you see him/her?

6. How have your friendships changed?

7. Construct a relationship circle. Put the names of people who are most important to you at or near the center.

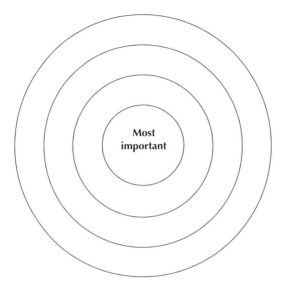

8. As you get older, is your role in the family changing? If yes, how?

Leisure

9. How often in an average month do you do these activities for fun?

    a. Go to a club/group meeting
    b. Go to a bar
    c. Go to a restaurant
    d. Go to a sports event
    e. Go to a shopping mall
    f. Go to a house of worship (e.g., church, synagogue, mosque)
    g. Talk with neighbors
    h. Go to a friend's house
    i. Go to a relative's house
    j. Go to a movie, play, or concert
    k. Play sports
    l. Go to a park
    m. Go to the library
    n. Other

10. What is your favorite activity?

11. Do you have enough money to do what you enjoy?

12. Compared with 5 years ago, do you do leisure activities *outside of your home* more or less often?

13. Which of the following leisure activities do you do *at home?* How often?

Watch television	Play video games
Play cards	Sew
Read or listen to audiobooks	Talk on the phone
Play board games	Garden
Listen to music on the radio	Bird watch
Do puzzles	Other _____

14. Usually, do you do activities by yourself or with others?

15. Do you have a close friend with whom you do activities?

16. If you want to do something special, do you have someone to do it with?

17. In your spare time, how often do you have nothing to do?

☐ Almost   ☐ Usually   ☐ Sometimes   ☐ Not   ☐ Never
always   usually

18. What has changed in the past 5 years?

19. If you could change anything about your leisure activities (fun time), what would it be?

20. Do you go on vacation?
    How often?
    With whom?
    What do you do?

21. Tell me about the places you have been. What did you like best?

Section V: Well-Being

1. Overall, how would you rate your happiness?

☐ Very   ☐ Happy   ☐ So so   ☐ More sad   ☐ Unhappy
happy   than happy

2. Do you feel sad often?

3. Is there someone who cares how you feel?

4. Do you get to do what you want to do?

5. Are you worried or anxious during the day?

6. Do you feel safe in your surroundings?

7. Do you wish you could stay in bed all day?

8. Do you feel useful?

9. Are you interested or excited in something?

10. Do you often feel pleased about accomplishing something?

11. Do you feel that you are welcome in your community?

12. Do you feel you have control over your life?

13. Compared with your friends, do you have more or fewer possessions?

14. What are the three most important things in your life?

15. Can you make your own decisions?

16. Are you happy with your living arrangements?

17. Have you had to cope with significant life events (e.g., births, deaths, family moves)?

18. Who or what has helped you through those events?

19. How do you go about solving problems?

20. Tell me about a typical day in your life (e.g., activities, times of activities, who helps).

21. Do weekends differ from weekdays?

22. Is your typical day different from 5 years ago?

23. What are your dreams?

24. What are your worries?

25. Look down the road 5 years. Tell me what you see.

26. What is the *best* thing that has happened to you in the past year.

27. What is the *worst* thing?

28. When you see young girls with disabilities today, what is different? What is the same?

29. What do you think is the secret to your life?

Index

Page numbers followed by *f* or *t* indicate figures or tables, respectively.